CAN YOU HEAR ME, GOD?

Vic Merrill

Exposition Press   *Smithtown, New York*

FIRST EDITION

© 1981 by Vic Merrill

ISBN 0-682-49740-1

Printed in the United States of America

*This book is dedicated
to my God source*

Contents

Preface   ix

1   Can You Hear Me, God?   1
2   Proving Myself   8
3   Just Not Ready for Girls Yet   13
4   A New Job   15
5   Wedding Bells   20
6   1933   23
7   "Good Night, Big Shot"   28
8   How Do You Know, Pat?   33
9   Maybe God Does Answer   37
10 Selling the Business   42
11 Just Know You Can Do It   45
12 The Healing Light   49
13 A New Business Venture   56
14 The Abundance of Life Is All About Us   61
15 Helping People   64
16 Lucky Me—Another Jackpot   68
17 Do You Know?   73
18 My Son Richard   76
19 I Love You   79
20 We Meet Again   82

Preface

A friend of mine once said, "Vic, why don't you write a book?" This was back in 1970. I said to him, "Me, write a book?" I thanked him for his idea, but didn't think much about it at that time.

It is now ten years later and I'm sure he'll be surprised, but pleased, when I tell him I have written the book he suggested I write.

In this book I have tried to relate to you, the reader, my actual experiences as to what I call my God source. They have brought about the unique method of communicating with the actual spirit forces that relate to the actual experiences that take place, fulfilling the needs of people in all walks of life.

You will find that my experiences will help you, the reader, to understand the simplicity of the knowing in your own mind, and how to help yourself bring about greater love and success in your own life.

It is possible some of you readers may have experienced some of the things I have written and recall them as you read.

I have written this book for myself, to recall some of the experiences of my life. By writing them, I had to relive them again, experience them again.

It has been fun for me and I hope it will be fun for you.

—VIC MERRILL

CAN YOU HEAR ME, GOD?

1

||||||||||||||||||||||||||||||||||||||||||||||||||||||||||||||||||||||||||||||||||||||||||||||||||||||||||||||||||||||||||||||||||

Can You Hear Me, God?

Yes, I, like millions of others, have reached out to God asking for help for myself or my family in times of need or illness. I have planted the seed, hoping for a good harvest, only to be left in silence, wondering.

"Can You hear me, God? My brother is dying—the cow is sick, God. Help the little lamb we have in the kitchen to live. God! You can't let them kill the little pony with the broken leg. It's all I got, God." But God was silent.

When I was twelve years old, I walked down the aisle in the church and gave my life to God. I was told to pray to Jesus.

"Jesus is love. He understands. He is the Son of God. He was crucified on the cross. He died for our sins. You were born a sinner. Ask Jesus to forgive you your sins."

I believed until . . .

One night in the middle of the night, I heard my mother crying. I tiptoed silently to the bedroom door and listened. I hardly breathed as they talked. I knew I would get a licking with a strap if my dad heard me.

Mother was sobbing, asking Dad, "How can we feed them? Where will we go? Will they take everything?"

"Yes," was his answer. "They will sell everything—the farm, all the stock, wagons—everything. The bank has gone broke. We cannot pay back the money we borrowed."

"When do we have to move?" asked my mother.

"When school is out, in about sixty days," replied Father.

The following night I heard Mother crying and praying: "God, help us. Show us the way." But God was silent.

Each night, I would kneel and ask Jesus to help Mother and Dad save the farm, the cows, the pigs, the big red rooster that woke us up in the morning. Then I thought of our new pony. We called him Mike. He was small, dark brown with a white face, and his tail almost touched the ground.

Our hearts were broken. My brother and my little sister just couldn't understand. One day, we kneeled under the big apple tree and prayed. I said, "God, have we sinned against You? Why don't You answer?" But God was silent.

I will never forget the day of the auction. We never realized how much we loved Bossie, the cow, and her baby calf until they put them in the auction ring. And the big red rooster with his flock of red hens; it was funny how he lorded over them. There was Nanny, the goat that we laughed at so many times as she chased us out of the barnyard.

I ran to Dad, asking, "Will they sell our new pony, Mike?"

"Yes, everything."

Then I cried as if my heart would break. He held me close and said, "We will find a place to live somewhere. God will show us the way."

I prayed to Jesus, saying, "Jesus, help us save the pony, Mike." But Jesus was silent.

I went out to the hayloft in the barn and screamed out as loud as I could. "God! Can You hear me? Save our pony!" But God was silent.

Mike was sold for only ten dollars. Only ten dollars, I thought. He was worth a hundred. We loved him so much.

The big red bull was next. He was mean and we hoped he would rush them as they opened the barn door. He surely would know something was wrong with all those people there. No, I guess not. He stood there like a gentleman in the ring. They paid so little for him.

Then there was the little burro. He was so funny. When someone got on him, or put a saddle on him, he would lie down. We called him Moses because Dad said he brayed like a preacher. Mother said that wasn't very nice of Dad. Moses brought only five dollars, saddle and all.

Oh, yes! I almost forgot Aunt Matilda. She was our little white hen. We called her Aunt Matilda because she cackled all the time.

That night after the auction was over, we sat under the big apple tree. No one spoke. We just sat there looking at the moon, the stars, and wondering, Can You hear us, God?

The night was hot. We were all too tired to get up to go into the house to go to bed. We spent the night there under the stars. The next morning the sun was bright and our old hound dog, Joseph, came around licking our faces, waking us up.

A man came walking toward us. My little sister sat up and asked Mamma, "Is that God?" No, he wasn't God, but maybe God had heard. He was a man I delivered milk to every evening in the little town five miles away where I went to school.

The man said, "I was at the auction yesterday, and last night I began to wonder where you folks were going to go, so something said to me to go see the Merrill family. I have a small house in town. It ain't much, but if you like, you folks can move in there for nothing until you get settled again." It seemed to me like he just kept saying, "It ain't much, but it's a place to go."

Then he looked at me and said, "There is a man down south of the town a little ways—about ten miles. His name is Jones and he's looking for a boy like you to work for the summer. Why don't you run down there and see?" Then he said, "You better take some extra clothes. I think he will like you." He looked at my mother and said, "He may not be back until September." Then he looked at my dad and said, "The mills in St. Joe are looking for men. Why don't you take the train there and I am sure you'll get a job—hard work, but it's a job."

Fifteen years old, a boy who had never been ten miles from home started down the road with a sack over his shoulder seeking a farmer by the name of Jones. I ran most of the way repeating,

"God, I've got to get that job. God, I've got to get that job." As I approached the farmhouse down the lane, I ran harder and didn't even feel tired.

I had arrived but could not think of what to do next. I didn't have to do anything. A man stepped out of the barn door and said, "What's your hurry, young feller?" All I could think of to say was "I've got to get that job." "It's hard work," he said. "I will work hard," I answered. "All right," he said, "the job is yours.

"Come, sit over here and I'll explain what has to be done. We get up at four A.M., feed and milk the cows, feed and harness the horses, then we go to the fields after eating breakfast—better eat a big breakfast—we don't stop for lunch, just lemonade and water. We quit at six, come in, unharness, then feed and milk the cows. Dinner is at eight o'clock.

"Now come. I'll show you the bunk house." As we approached the bunker, he stopped and said, "No, it's full. I forgot."

My heart dropped so hard if it had been a rock it would have crushed my foot. I thought he, or someone else, had hired another man and he had forgotten.

We stood there silent for a moment. Then he said, "Come with me. Bring your sack. We have a big room in the attic." As we went through the kitchen, he said, "What's your name, boy?" "Vic is my name, sir." "Well, Vic, this is my wife, Sarah." About that time, a young girl stepped through the door from the stairway. The man said, "Vic, this is Linda, my wife's niece from over the hill. She is helping out here, too."

We climbed the stairs to the attic. There was a bed, an old dresser, and, best of all, a large window that opened to the roof facing the south. He told me, "You can watch the moon come up from there." I had already thought of lying out there to look at the moon and count the stars.

It was noontime. As we went through the kitchen on our way out of the house, Sarah called to me, "Vic, I have some hot soup for you. Just sit there." As I sat down, Linda came in and sat down. She proceeded to ask me a lot of silly questions. "Where do you live? How old are you? Where do you go to school?" I was tall for my age, so I said, "Sixteen." "Oh," she said, "I'm sixteen, too!" I remained silent, only answering her when I had to.

After I ate the soup the boss took me out to the barn and handed me a pitchfork, pointed to the horse manure and said, "Throw it out the window."

I worked hard and fast, wanting to do a good job. About four o'clock Linda appeared with a large glass of lemonade. "You're working too hard," she said, "slow down, drink this." I was sure glad for the lemonade and thanked her, but I began to wonder about this girl. Oh, she was pretty, lovely blond hair, tall and thin, but I had no experience with girls and I didn't want to start now.

About nine o'clock all the chores had been taken care of and dinner was over, so I went to my room and flopped on the bed. I soon fell fast asleep with the thought of thank you, God! Thank you, God!

It seemed like such a short night. Mr. Jones rapped on the door and called, "Let's go, Vic!" I had been dreaming I was in a new world and Linda was with me. My first thought was, no, no! I don't want a girlfriend.

I dressed quickly and ran down the stairs to follow Mr. Jones to the barn. He said, "Well, we beat the other men out here. You're going to do all right." He made me feel good. Three other men came to the barn and Mr. Jones told me their names were Peter, Harry, and John.

When we went to breakfast, Linda was there. She said, "Good morning, Vic." I managed to mumble, "Good morning."

The day went fast and by 9:15 that evening, I was on the roof looking at the moon and counting the stars. My mother, my little sister, and my brother all seemed to be there with me and I knew that all was well. That was Thursday night and I thought, Friday, Saturday, then Sunday and I can go home.

Sunday, I was tired and slept until noontime, so I didn't go home. When I went down the stairs, Linda was there fixing my breakfast. As I ate, she talked and talked. After I finished, I went outside and sat under the big oak tree just to rest. Still confused by the loss of our home and all the animals I loved, I sat lost in thought. Linda slipped out of the house and sat down beside me. I didn't even feel her presence until she spoke to me. I was miles away and I almost jumped a few more.

She asked, "Do you want to walk? I have something to show you." We walked together and soon came upon a small nest of six baby quail. It was too much! I began to sob and walked over to a log to sit down. Linda could not understand. "What's wrong?" she asked. I was embarrassed—so embarrassed! Cry before a girl?

Linda was a persistent girl and soon had me talking about our home and the auction. I was glad. I know I had found a friend, even if it was a girl. We spent many evenings together on the roof. She kept sitting closer to me. Then, one evening, she came with so little on that I was embarrassed. She sat so close to me that before I knew it, I was having the most pleasant experience of my life. From then on, I had a new and special regard for girls.

Thirty days passed with no word from home. I began to say, "God, is everything all right?" Then one Saturday, Mr. Jones asked, "Vic, would you like to go home?" "Would I!" I replied. "We are going to town," he said, "and you can ride in with us, then run back on Sunday. Sarah and Linda are also going along."

I found my mother, my brother, and my little sister still in the house that was offered to us by that wonderful man who found us sleeping on the lawn. Dad had gotten the job at the mill and all was well. Mother said they were all going to move there when they could get the money. I wanted to help Mother, but I didn't know how much or when Mr. Jones would pay me. I asked God to help him to be fair with me. I felt that God had blessed me in many ways and I sure did not want to get on the wrong side of Him. So why shouldn't I trust Mr. Jones, I thought.

As the sun was setting, I hugged them all goodbye, telling them I would be back at the end of August, in thirty long days. I left and ran all the way back—anxious to see Linda, but Linda was not there. Sarah told me that she had gone home, as she was needed by her parents. I never heard from her again. There were times at night when I would wake up thinking she was softly kissing my lips. But no, no, it was not supposed to be. It seemed as if God had taken her away.

Then I began to think, "God, did You take our farm and all the animals away? God, did You take Linda away like the farm? Why, God? Why?" But God was silent. I never sat on the roof again.

It seemed as if the end of the month would never come. But that day did come and Mr. Jones handed me a check for ninety dollars. I could hardly hold back the tears, as it was more than Mother needed to pay the movers for taking our furniture to St. Joe.

I told Sarah and Mr. Jones goodbye, thanked them, and started running the ten miles home with the good-news check. The moving men came the next day, loaded up everything we had, and we were ready to leave.

The little house was empty now and I thought I should go thank the man who had been so kind to us. When I knocked on the door, he came out, greeting me warmly. I thanked him for the use of his house and for also telling us about the jobs for Dad and myself. He looked puzzled and said, "1 don't have a little house over there. I did not come to your house." What could I say? We had all seen him with our own eyes. All I could say, was, "Well, it looked like you. Thank you and goodbye."

As I ran back, I said, "God, can You hear me? It was You, God. It was You, wasn't it?" But God was silent.

I never told Mother and the other children. All the way to St. Joe I could not help but think of God. Does He always come when you need Him, but never speak? I don't know, God. I just don't understand. Maybe we had to learn a lesson the hard way.

2

Proving Myself

St. Joseph, Missouri, September 5, fifteen years old. School would be starting the following Monday. I was scared to death. How will I manage this, God? If only I could be lucky enough to play basketball, I might be able to make a few friends and be accepted.

I signed up and three days later the coach called me in and asked me how much I had played. When I told him he just smiled and asked me where I was from. "Down on the farm," I said, "and I'm pretty damn good. If you'll give me a chance I'll prove it to you." "You're pretty small, it gets rough out there," he cautioned. "Give me five minutes on the court, I don't care how rough they are," I answered. He just looked at me for a moment, then called a couple of players over and told them to guard me. He threw me the ball and said, "See if you can make a basket or two, Vic." I thought, God, I sure need your help now. Well, it was easy. I made five baskets in five minutes. They never got hold of the ball. I was fast. When the coach blew the whistle and called me over he just said, "You are damn good. Report for practice tomorrow." It was a great day; I was happy and on the way home I said, "Thanks, God. I'll do my best."

School was hard for me that fall. I was known as the farmerboy. I was different from them and they were different from me, but on the basketball court I was their hero. We only lost one game that fall season. It was hard for me to understand why they

8

loved me on the ball court but passed me by in other areas of the school.

At Christmas vacation time I knew I would be unable to return to school. Dad worked only three days a week at the mill. There was no unemployment paycheck or food stamps. You worked or you didn't eat. So at night I talked to God. What can a farm boy do in the city, God? I have to find work. Where shall I go? It was three days later when I walked into the office of a large candy factory. I just stood there for fifteen minutes. I didn't know what to do. In my mind I kept saying, God, what shall I do?

Then a kind man came up and asked, "Can I help you?" I smiled and asked for work. "Where are you from, boy?" he asked. "Down on the farm, sir," I told him. "We lost the farm and everything; the bank went broke. I need a job and I'll work hard." He just stood there for two or three minutes, then he looked up and said, "You come in tomorrow morning at eight o'clock and ask for me, Mr. Chase. I'm the owner." "Thank you, Mr. Chase." As soon as I stepped outside the building I thanked God.

Now as I write and think back over the experiences I have had, either God or some God source had to be helping me. Years later, when I employed a lot of people, I had kindness in my heart for those who needed a job.

I was one happy boy when I arrived home, and Mother knew from the expression my face something good had happened. We all sat around the big oak kitchen table and they listened while I told them about the kind man Mr. Chase and my new job.

That night I heard Mother thanking God for our good fortune, and once again, I said, "God, can You hear me? Thank you, God."

But God was silent.

I reported to the factory early the next morning rather nervous as to what they might have me do and whether I would be able to do a good job. I sat on a bench seat for a while waiting for Mr. Chase. A nice lady came by and said, "Mr. Chase comes in at 8:15." She was right. At 8:15 Mr. Chase walked through the front door and said, "Good morning, Vic, come with me."

He walked briskly through the plant (I had never seen so many people in one place). Then we stopped in an area where two young fellows were making packing cartons. He called to one, Mr. Johnson, and said, "This is Vic. You will show him what to do in this department." Johnson stuck out his hand and welcomed me. Mr. Chase said that was all. "Thanks, Mr. Chase, thanks," I said. I doubt if he knew how grateful I was.

The next morning when I reported to work, the other man was not there. Mr. Johnson said they needed him in another department. "Vic," he said, "we have always needed three men here to keep up." He just stood there shaking his head and wondering how he would keep up with the flow of boxed chocolates coming down the chute.

I could feel the situation he was in, but didn't know what to do about it or what to expect. Thirty seconds later boxes of chocolates hit the chute and on to the revolving belt in a continuous flow. I seemed to know exactly what to do, and fast. Ten minutes later the belt was empty; all the boxes had been put in cartons and sealed. Mr. Johnson walked over, put his hand on my shoulder and said, "You're going to be all right." The third man never did come back. Three days later Mr. Chase walked by and asked how I was doing in this department. Mr. Johnson smiled and told him, "You can forget that third man. We don't need him." Mr. Chase just smiled and walked on.

God must have known this was the place for me, because Johnson (I had dropped the "Mr." by now) asked me to go to the young men's Bible Class at the Christian Church. I was very happy to be invited and accepted the invitation.

In the middle of the fall season at school I had learned that the minister from our little town who baptized me had moved to St. Joseph and we could find him at the Methodist Church. One day after school my brother and I went to see him. He was surprised to see us but not at all glad. He suggested that we find another church closer to our home.

I got the feeling he thought we were too poor to be in his church. That night as I lay on my bed I said once again, "God, can You hear me? Our old minister friend does not want us in his church. Do city clothes make that much difference?" It was confusing and hard to understand both God and the preacher.

At the Christian Church they had an indoor basketball court and I was permitted to practice in the evenings. Within thirty days I was playing basketball with the second team.

I began to feel good about myself. I had money to give to Mother and buy new clothes. Time moved quickly. I spent all my spare time shooting baskets and running the hundred-yard dash down the railroad tracks.

When the fall season opened I was playing ball with the first practice team, who had worked with the National Championship winners the past season. They were supported by the large Hyllard Chemical Company and were a beautiful professional team.

My first tryout with them was satisfactory, and I was chosen to play forward. When the first ball was tossed in the air I said, "God, I need Your help now."

It seemed like a perfect game. I couldn't miss a basket. At the end of the third quarter we were ten points ahead, but the fourth quarter was a big disaster for me. I had the ball, was running fast, when somehow one of the other players tripped me by accident. I hit my head on one of the other players, breaking my nose, pushing it out at the top in splinters, also losing some of my front teeth. I fell unconscious, but remember saying, "God! God, this is my time." Then I blacked out completely and knew nothing or heard nothing for three days and nights. The fourth morning, I woke up as if nothing had happened. Mother was sitting by my side, and said softly, "Vic, can you hear me?" I smiled at her and she knew all was well. She had been sitting there all three days and nights asking God to help me.

The next day Mr. Chase from the factory came in to see me. He called Mother to the side when he left and told her he had paid the hospital bill as well as the doctor bill. He, too, believed in God. I don't think he ever went to church, but it made no difference to me, as I knew the Church is not the only place to find God.

I was back to work in two weeks, and was I ever glad! I didn't realize how many friends this boy from the country had made in two and a half years working at the factory. However, I was still shy, especially around girls—a soft-spoken person with a big smile.

3

Just Not Ready for Girls Yet

Time changes people. I did not look like the boy from the country who first came to the city. I was growing up, well dressed in city clothes, and had greater confidence in myself. I had begun to shave. I looked the part, and Mother often reminded me that I would be successful some day.

The girls began to notice me and I enjoyed looking at them. I remember while going to school that past fall in St. Joe, there was a sweet girl my age, black hair, long flashing eyelids, blue eyes, and a very intriguing smile. She seemed perfect. She was my biggest rooter at the basketball games. I liked her very much, but I never asked her out. I was not at ease with girls then.

She caught up with me one evening when I was taking a walk up to the bluff overlooking the Missouri River. I wanted to be alone, to talk the God, but she said, "I'm going with you." We walked and talked about school and life and wondered what would happen to us in the future. I told her she was very pretty and I liked her, but my only desire now was to find a good job so that I could help my mother and family. I told her about the farm and life with the animals, which seemed to me like they all lived within the laws of nature. Even the grain in the fields and the green grass we were sitting on lived harmoniously together. Only man seems to have problems finding a way to live his life in harmony and love, and in competing with others for jobs.

She asked why I would not go out with her. She said she wanted to be my girl, then said, "I will do anything you like."

Then she stood up and hoisted her dress up over hips and said, "See, I don't have any underclothes on. I will be yours now." I was embarrassed, as she stood there in the light of the moon. Then I began to realize what she was trying to tell me. She was lonesome, she wanted a friend to share with because school was not easy for her. The other girls shunned her.

I took her by the hand and sat her down beside me, embracing her as she cried. I tried to tell her there wasn't anything wrong with her. I just wasn't ready for girls and if I was she would be the one I would choose. We sat and talked through the night. I learned from her that girls and women have secret lovers in their imaginations. They often fall in love with movie actors or someone they admire, even after marriage. This was hard for me to believe. I had never heard of such ideas or dreams. Then she said, "You will always be my lover because I admire you and often dream of you."

As we sat there sharing life with each other, we both realized that the sun had begun to peek over the hills. We rushed home to find that the police and others were starting to search for us. We tried to tell them where we had been all night and that we were just talking. I don't think anyone believed us, but it was true and all was well between the two of us. She became my best friend and that night taught me to have a high regard for young girls.

A few weeks later, she found a nice boyfriend and seemed happy, but she always called me her lover.

Fifteen years later, she saw me and ran to me saying, "There is my lover." I was glad when she threw her arms around me and said, "Vic, Vic, how are you?" Her husband just stood by and looked.

I tell you of these experiences hoping that you will understand we learn most by the experience we go through in life.

I will never forget that night I spent with such a lovely girl, sitting on the bluff of the river sharing with each other.

Maybe you, too, remember back to such an experience and can relive the joy that brought an understanding to your heart.

4

A New Job

Spring had turned into summer and I always enjoyed the three-mile walk home after work. I seemed to enjoy all nature and the love that was within everything. Something seemed to be telling me that it was time to look for a new job.

One evening as I walked through the retail clothing area I saw a brand-new Buick parked in the street. A man was wiping the dust off with a cloth. I stopped, and stood there looking. To me it was the most beautiful car I had ever seen. It was dark blue with varnished wood spoke wheels and a trunk in the back. The upholstery was so very soft and beautiful. I thought the man must be very rich. He spoke to me, saying, "How do you like it?" My answer was "Beautiful, just beautiful." "I just bought it and like to keep it wiped off," he replied. Then he told me he owned the Florsheim shoe store there.

All kinds of thoughts went through my mind: shoes, new car, money. It must be wonderful. Why, I'll never know, but I said to him, "I will come in and clean your store for free if you will teach me how to sell shoes. I have dress clothes." He stood there pondering my offer. I wondered if God was speaking to him as he stood there silent. Then he said, "It's a pretty big job, come let me show you." He spent one hour showing me the work that had to be done. Then he talked about shoes. He took great pride in the store and seemed to be pleased that I listened to every word. He asked, "Do you want to start tomorrow evening?" "Sure, I'll try hard to please," I answered. "All right, he said, "you can clean in the evening and then come in on Saturday and we will teach you how to sell shoes and relate to customers." It was hard for me to tell Mr. Chase at the candy factory that I had a new job and would be leaving them. His remarks were "Good, I am pleased. I have been thinking about you lately, wondering about a better job for you. But this change is good. I am pleased."

During the weeks ahead many of the factory workers came to the store and purchased shoes, which pleased the store owner.

Six months passed fast and I was happy. We moved to a better house in a nicer area of the city. Mother took in two boarders, a young man and his wife. They were so much in love with each other, I thought God must be pleased. Dad got a better job and we were able to save a little money.

Many times in the night I became very silent, then said, "God, can You hear me? This is Vic! Thank You, God, all is well." But, as usual, God was silent.

All was well at the shoe store except for one thing—the boss's daughter. I was invited to his house one evening for dinner. When we entered the house there stood the most lovely girl I had ever seen. She had long blond hair and blue eyes. When she walked toward me my eyes moved from the top of her head to her toes. My thoughts seemed to ask if she was real. My boss said, "Vic, this is Jeanie, our daughter." Then his wife walked in and she, too, was a very lovely lady. I asked him how one man could be so lucky. He laughed and said, "Positive thinking." His statement came to my mind many times—positive thinking. We had many talks later about positive thinking and believing in oneself. I told him I believed in God and talked to Him often, but he never answered.

I just wiped Jeanie out of my mind, because I thought they were too rich for me and she must have already had a boyfriend. However, the next week I was invited over again for dinner and a long ride in the new Buick. Jeanie and I sat in the back seat.

The invitations came more often and I found myself falling in love with Jeanie. It took me a while to realize Jeanie was also falling in love with me. I also began to realize she was looking for a husband and her father was on her side. The new Buick did have a big influence on me, but I couldn't see myself getting married. I began to ask myself why. Why, God? How can I get out of this situation? Although God was silent, there were times when I thought God was laughing and saying, "There is Vic all wrapped up with a girl again."

I got in deeper and deeper with Jeanie and she was thinking more of marriage. She was so lovely and fun to be with, but memories of Mother crying in the night asking God how they could feed the family, put them through school and buy clothes made me afraid of the responsibility.

One day a man walked into the store. The boss introduced him and said he was a district manager for Florsheim. He told me they needed a person like me in their big Kansas City store. He asked me if I would consider moving there. It was a shock to me. I had seen this man before, but never met him. My boss said, "Vic, we don't want to lose you, but it's a nice promotion and a big raise. I will leave the decision up to you."

That night I lay on my bed and said, "God, can You hear me?" God was silent. There was the family and Jeanie—what about them? What a big decision to make! However, the next morning I knew I would go to Kansas City.

The following weekend I told the family goodbye. The boss and Jeanie took me to the train station. We held each other closely and cried. We promised to write and I told her I would come back on the third weekend.

The store in Kansas City was a beautiful place to work. It was Kansas City's finest men's and women's clothing store, with a large Florsheim shoe department. Their motto was "Satisfy the Customer." My boss had taught me well, and the people soon accepted me as one of the group.

Friday evening on the second weekend just before closing time, I looked up toward the front door and thought Jeanie was walking in. She was too far away for me to see, so I decided it couldn't be her. I turned my attention to a customer looking at our display of shoes. A few moments later someone touched my back and said, "Hello, Vic." What a surprise! It was Jeanie. We hugged each other right there in front of the customers and all. It was so good to see someone from home. She stayed two nights with me, and when I put her on the train for home I said to myself, Yes, Jeanie, I will marry you. I think she knew it.

Two weeks later I went home to see the family and Jeanie. They were all so nice to me. Mother always fixed my favorite food—fried chicken and mashed potatoes. I called a few of the fellows that I played basketball with and we reminisced over the games we played together. They were always so kind.

It was hard to leave Jeanie when I left to go back to Kansas City. We arrived at the train station early and sat on a wooden bench, just being silent. I wondered if God was with us.

Two weeks later at closing time Jeanie walked in the store again. She looked lovelier than ever. She filled my being with excitement. I was so glad to see her again so soon.

That night we went to the Playmore Ball Room and danced until midnight, hardly saying a word. We were so close to each other and loved each other so. But there was something different about Jeanie that night, something mysterious. I asker her about it and she laughed and said, "No, I'm the same as yesterday." The next day we talked about marriage, life, love, and children. She wanted a girl, then a boy, then another girl.

I told her I was afraid of measuring up to the responsibility of a family. I told her about the farm and Mother crying in the night and asking God for help to care for the family. I asked her to help me overcome my fear. She just said, "We can work it out."

Sunday evening when she boarded the train, there was that mysterious smile. I didn't mention it, but I knew something was happening to Jeanie. That night when all was quiet I said, "God, can You hear me? What's happening to Jeanie?" But God was silent.

A week later I received a letter from her saying, "Vic, I love you very much. The past few nights I have been lying awake thinking. Something keeps saying it will not work out, it will not not work out."

She went on to say it would be hard for her to leave her family, her work and friends. Then she said, "Forgive me, Vic, I love you very much, but I think it best to end our relationship for a while. Let's wait and see. Give me a little time."

That night I shared my feelings with God. "Why?" I asked. "Why? Did You have anything to do with Jeanie, God?' But God was silent.

I didn't return to St. Joe for a month. I just didn't feel like going, but a note from Mother said, "Come home, Vic, I need to talk."

That weekend I went home. I walked from the train station all the way home. Everything seemed so silent. I was in a different world,, for there were no memories of the past, no thoughts about anything or anyone. When I walked up the stairs at home, Mother opened the door and greeted me with "Hi, Vic." Then we hugged each other and just stood there for a few moments. Then she spoke, saying, "I just had to see you, Vic. What has happened, Vic? You're not the happy person I once knew." I had to tell her about Jeanie. We cried, and we laughed. Then she said, "God will work it out."

Sunday afternoon I called Jeanie. Her first statement was "Vic, are you all right? When can I pick you up, Vic? I want to see you!" It was so good to be in each other's arms, but there was that mysterious smile again and she still claimed she knew nothing about it. That evening she took me to the train station. When saying goodbye she told me again she just had to wait and see. We promised to keep in touch. We wrote each other often for about six months. Her letters often expressed her thoughts of life and love, her family and friends. We learned so much, sharing with each other. The letters seemed to have a positive attitude, a beautiful understanding. Then her last letter said, "Vic, I have someone else. I love him very much. We will be married soon."

Somehow I knew she would find another and all was well. My answer to her was a wish for her happiness and a blessing of love. That night I asked God to bless her and love her, and to help me never get involved with another girl.

5

···

Wedding Bells

The days and nights were long for the next three months. I turned my attention to work and I thanked God for it.

In the months ahead I made many customer friends, mostly women, young and old. Somehow I seemed to have a rapport with them. Many of them would come and ask me to select gifts, such as shirts and ties, for their husbands. Once a middle-aged lady asked me to help her select some ties, which took about two hours and my boss was getting a little upset. Also, I didn't know the president of the store was watching. After the lady left, he came over to me and asked, "Who was that lady, Vic?" I told him her name was Mrs. Long. "What did she buy?" he asked. "One hundred five-dollar ties," I told him. Then he turned to my boss and said, "Mrs. Long is one of the richest ladies in Kansas City." I didn't know what to expect, for my boss was angry and I had never had any conversations with the president. I was a bit scared. My thoughts went to God—"God, am I in trouble?" I asked. The next statement from the president was "Vic, you assist any person that needs helps in this store." Then he turned to my boss and said, "You had better find another salesman for this department. I see we'll be able to use Vic wherever we need him."

After that I was hopping all over the store. Some of the ladies would come to me for my advice about the new dress they had on and were about to purchase. I never lied to them. I seemed to have a taste and love for clothes. There were times when I would put my hands over my eyes and say, "Take it off, take it off—you have better taste than that."

I was happy, but, at the same time, saddened. I had no church and no God that I could feel. No relationship with nature. Just my work. I thought God was there, but He was alway silent.

One evening when I arrived at the boarding house where I lived, I was introduced to a young fellow by the name of Dale Smith. He was a nice-looking quiet person with a nice smile. We liked each other and more so when he told me he was a shoe salesman at a Florsheim store in the south part of the city.

The weekends were long for me and I dreaded Sundays. There were many invitations from friends at the store, but I desired to be alone.

One Saturday night Dale asked me to go to the Playmore Ball Room. I hadn't been there since the night when Jeanie and I were together there. I went, and Dale and I continued to go almost every Saturday night and on Sunday afternoons for almost a year.

We didn't ask anyone for a date. We just went to dance. I did meet a sweet blond girl and we often danced together during the year. She had studied dancing and it was a real treat for me to dance with her.

She was a quiet person, but had a big smile with big dimples and was smart as a fox. Her name was Reven. I never asked her to go out.

Dale had a car, and we were planning to go home to St. Joe the following Sunday. I asked Reven if she would like to ride along. She gave me a big ha-ha.

About one month later at the Ball Room she said, "Vic, I would like to ride along the next time you go to see your mother." Well, that same girl Reven is my wife today. We dated for a year. Our being together seemed natural, no big deal, just a beautiful relationship, an understanding of each other. I asked God, "Is this the one?" God was silent. Not a yes or no.

We planned to have the wedding at Reven's church in Kansas City, but Mother couldn't come, so we changed it to the Christian

Church in St. Joe. It was on a Saturday afternoon. We invited a few friends, but somehow the news got out and just before the ceremony started about thirty young fellows marched in and sat down. I was so filled with joy and love I could hardly hold back the tears. They were the ones I played basketball with in the same church.

One never knows who their real friends are until there is a need, or their presence counts. Their presence reminded me to let my actions speak instead of my words.

I often wondered if this is the way God works, in silence, but always present when there is a real need.

In the late hours of the morning I would wake up, and in the silence I often thought I was being blessed by an unknown source. It seemed like they were trying to tell me something. I did not know about the spirits inside the body or those that surround the outside of the body from the time we are born until we lay the body down to return to the earth.

6

‖‖

1933

In the spring we purchased a new automobile. It was an Auburn Facton sedan. It reminded me of my former boss's Buick. Our first trip was to St. Joe to see the family and show them the new car. Mother was just elated and enjoyed a ride out in the country.

Later that afternoon, I drove down to the Florsheim store to say hello to my old boss. We were so glad to see each other. He had heard that I was doing well at the store in Kansas City and he was happy and pleased with the new car sitting in front of his store. We seemed to have a father-son relationship and I felt that he wished I was his son-in-law. As we sat there talking, Jeanie walked in. We just looked at each other, not knowing what to say. Then we reached for each other, holding each other closely. The tears were running down her cheeks. My boss left. I think he had a few tears, too. After we regained our composure we sat down and talked. I told her I had been married about a year. She told me about her little girl and her husband. Almost an hour had passed, when the boss returned with his wife. Then the tears flowed again. She was such a lovely lady. When I left, Jeanie walked out to the car and gave me a big hug and said, "Vic, I still read your letters. I will always be in love with you. I am happy, but unhappy on the inside. Bless you, Vic. Goodbye."

I never saw her again, nor heard from her. But the memories come back to me often and I ask God, "Are we supposed to learn from these experiences? Is our life preplanned when we are born?" God was silent.

That summer I had two weeks' vacation and made plans to drive out to California. Reven had relatives in Los Angeles, and my older sister lived in Northern California. We took Mother and my younger sister along. It was our honeymoon.

What a great experience for me! I had never seen the ocean, an orange grove, or a desert. In fact, I had never been over one hundred miles from where I was born. The beauty of it all seemed like a whole new world to me. We swam in the ocean, we ate tons of oranges and green lettuce, artichokes, cracked crab—so many things. We drove and drove, seeing the sights, and I saw my first baseball game. Everyone was so kind to us. Mother was so happy.

A week had passed and we were going to leave the next morning to visit my sister in Stockton. However, that evening my sister and brother-in-law drove up. It was a great surprise. They came down just to be with us on the way to Stockton. They were driving an Auburn just like ours, except a different color. Though it was a fast trip to Stockton we had an enjoyable time. The next day Ted said, "There isn't much to see in Stockton, so let's go to San Francisco. We'll spend the night there so we'll have plenty of time to see much of the city."

When we arrived at the ferryboat, we drove the car inside, got out and walked up to the passenger deck. I could hardly believe what I was seeing. Reven had been there before and often stood looking at the expression on my face.

Crossing the bay on a ferryboat for the first time was one of the greatest moments of my life. Riding the cable cars was another, and eating at the wharf still another. I just fell in love with San Francisco. My thoughts went back to the farm and I thought how fortunate I was now. I often said, "Thank You, God, for such a beautiful experience." I was never one to say long prayers to God.

It was 6:00 A.M. Friday when we said goodbye. My younger sister stayed with my sister and brother-in-law. She never returned to St. Joe.

We had three days to drive the 2,000 miles back to St. Joe, then on to Kansas City. It was a long way, but the beauty that surrounded us kept us so inspired we needed little sleep. The drive over the mountains to Reno was tremendous, then Salt Lake City, Denver, then across the flat lands to St. Joe and Kansas City. Then we were home again. There is no place like home to rest a few hours and reflect back over the past.

Monday morning, back to work and stories about our trip. Business was slow that day. It was good because so many wanted to know about our trip. I wondered if God had anything to do with it.

The next three years passed quickly and smoothly. We danced at the Playmore Ball Room quite a lot and spent more time with Mother and the family.

Reven's mother was wonderful. She liked me and I liked her. She was much fun to be with and so easy to please.

The following year my brother-in-law and sister went to Detroit to pick up a new car. On the way home they stopped by to see us. Both of them insisted that we move to California. It brought back memories of San Francisco. When they arrived home they wrote asking us to come. "You just have to move out here to be with us," they said.

Nine months later we packed our car and headed for California. It was a hard decision to make. I loved my job, but I felt like making a change. I often said, "God, am I doing the right thing?" But as we came closer and closer to California I was sure I had made the right choice.

It was real fun being with my sister and brother-in-law again in Stockton. After a week's rest I told them it was time I looked for a job. There didn't seem to be much in the way of my kind of work in Stockton, so I went to San Francisco. The stores were big there but I found no work the first day. That night in my hotel room I said, "God, I need your help. I need a job." The next day at the Florsheim store I asked and they said, no, they didn't need anyone.

I showed them my letter of recommendation and said, "If you will give me an equal turn with the other salesmen and customers I will work Thursday, Friday, and Saturday for nothing if I don't sell more than each one of your salesmen." The manager read my letters again, then said, "I can't lose on that, can I?" He was still leery of my offer and maybe leery of me, but when I told him I would treat each customer with respect and the utmost care he said, "Come in tomorrow at nine A.M."

At closing time Saturday evening I knew I was ahead when the manager said, "You come in Monday morning; I like the way you work."

I had a job. That night I called Reven and told her the good news. She came down a few days later and found us a place to live in San Francisco.

I find that lots of people will say no in many areas of business, especially to sales people. It's easier to say no than yes. If they say no they can change their mind like the store manager I asked for a job. I had to convince him with action instead of words.

This same principle applies today. If you are out of work or want to make a change, make sure you know what you want to do, then pick out the company you would like to work for, go see them and tell them you want to work for them and why.

Now don't, don't ask what the hours are, what they pay, how many weeks' vacation, sick leave, how long before you get a raise. If you really want a job with that company, forget all about the above questions and tell them if they can fit you in any place, you will work your tail off to prove your ability to perform. You may shock everyone, but I'll bet you ten to one you will get a job. Many large companies are seeking people with a drive to get ahead, and promotion will come if your thinking is right.

Abundance—it's there in these large companies, also smaller ones, but you have to work for it. Just learn to love yourself and everyone else, be happy, and soon you will discover a new person within and you will be pleased with yourself. Always remember you are you. You are a part of this great intelligent force of God. Quit putting yourself down, quit trying to be somebody else. Be grateful for you.

After nine months at the shoe store I had had it. I was unhappy, as they lacked imagination and had no interest in what they were doing. I discussed this with the manager and we decided it was best I resign.

Arriving at home that evening I found Reven very solemn. I guess she was making plans in her mind. Before I told her I had quit my job she asked me to sit beside her and hold her hand. She wanted to tell me the good news.

We sat a moment and she just said, "I am pregnant." I could only think of one thing: "How long have you been pregnant?" "Two months," she said. I didn't have the courage to tell her I had quit my job. I couldn't think of anything to say. We just sat there, both silent. Then I thought, "God, can You hear me? Reven is going to have a baby." God was silent, but He must have heard, as I got a beautiful feeling of peace. I reached over and put my arms around her, kissing her as tenderly as I knew how. "Okay, it's okay, we'll have the baby," I said.

All the fear of having a family was wiped away when I told God Reven was having a baby. That night I asked God to make it a girl.

The next morning when we woke she snuggled over close and asked, "Does it make any difference if it's a boy or a girl?" "Yes, yes!" I said. "I want a girl." No more was said. (It *was* a girl— a beautiful, curly brown-headed girl.) I could not tell her I had quit my job. I dressed and left as if I were going to work.

7

"Good Night, Big Shot"

As I drove downtown I asked, "God, can You hear me? What will I do now that Reven is going to have a baby? I quit my job, God, what now?" But God was silent. No answer—no answer.

When I approached the downtown area something seemed to tell me to find an employment agency. Yes, an agency might help, I thought. The interview was long, but good, although they did not offer me a job or much hope. I left with a long face. Not looking where I was going I bumped into a very lovely lady. The books and papers she was carrying hit the floor. I apologized and helped her pick them up. She took one look at me and asked, "What's wrong with you?" I don't know why, but I answered, "I quit my job, my wife is pregnant and my bank account is low." She laughed and asked if I had filled out an application. "Yes," I said, "I had an interview with that gentleman there, Mr. Morse." "Come with me," she said. I thought, Well, what now?

She picked up the application and took me to her office. I noticed the sign on the office door said "Manager." What a lovely manager! I thought.

We sat in silence for a while, then she picked up her phone and called a client. "I have a young fellow I think will more than fill your requirements for the job you are trying to fill." She kept saying, "Yes, yes, yes." I could not hear his questions, but as she hung up she looked at me and smiled. She wrote out his name on a piece of paper and said, "You meet this man at the St. Francis

28

Hotel for lunch at 11:45. Meet him at the reservation desk in the main dining room."

I smiled. It was a new day again for me. "I sure am glad I knocked those books and papers out of your hands." She handed me her card and said, "My name is Pat, the company will pay the fee." I took her hand, bent over and kissed her on the cheek, telling her how grateful I was. She was a little bit astonished, but said, "Vic, call me after the interview. I would like to know the outcome, because I think the job is yours."

I had an hour and forty-five minutes to kill. During that time many thoughts went through my mind. Pat did not tell me and I did not ask exactly what the job was. She just said it was a very sophisticated promotion program. He arrived on time and greeted me warmly, saying, "Now you follow me and listen."

First he contacted the maître d' and asked if all arrangements had been made. His answer was yes. Next he asked the cigarette girl to stand outside the dining room when the maître d' asked her to. Then he handed her five bucks and asked the maître d' to seat us at our table. He waited for him to pull the chairs out and seat us as if we were someone real imporant. After we were seated he handed me a card. It read: "Pall Mall Cigarettes. Where particular people congregate you'll find Pall Mall." Then he said, "Pat thinks you are the man for this job. How do you want your business cards to read?" Just as if the job was mine and I would accept it. He waited until the people had been served, then he motioned the maître d' to proceed. He walked to our table first. A tall black man dressed in a white uniform carried a large silver tray. On the tray were rows of full packages of Pall Mall cigarettes, arranged one high all facing up so when he turned the tray we could see a solid tray filled with Pall Mall cigarettes perfectly lined up. Each had a card on top like the one Mr. Epple had handed me. "Pall Mall Cigarettes. Where particular people congregate you'll find Pall Mall." The maître d' handed each of us a package, then made the rounds to each table, giving each one a package of Pall Malls. As he handed each one to the people he would say, "Compliments of the management."

After we finished our lunch he brought the check. He paid in cash for our lunch and each package of Pall Mall cigarettes he gave away. He also handed the maître d' $5.00 for the man carrying the tray and $10.00 for the maître d'. "Now," he said, "you are to become a very important man. For the next twelve months you will live in one of the major hotels from Bakersfield to Eureka, California, and the Riverside Hotel in Reno. Your day will start by ordering breakfast in your room. The waiter will arrange your breakfast from the tray to your table. Then he will present you with a package of Pall Mall cigarettes. He should present it just as they did here. If he does it properly, you thank him and tip him $2.00. If he does not, correct him. Everything has to be done properly, as we will be dealing with business executives and high society. Anyone ordering breakfast in their room will receive a package of Pall Malls presented by compliments of the management. After breakfast you will go to the waiter's quarters and explain how important it is to present Pall Mall properly. Then you will tip each one $2.00 and thank them on behalf of Pall Mall."

He talked for two hours, explaining in detail all phases of the program. Each day I was to invite some executive for lunch in one of the major hotels, and each night I was to have someone from business or society in one of the dining rooms. The same procedure would be followed, presenting Pall Mall cigarettes. He handed me a list of the hotels, which consisted of eight. Then he said, "Guess you will have to have two breakfasts some days and two lunches. Better work Saturdays in the evening." He handed me a list of instructions to study, a very comprehensive list of businessmen, and a list of those in high society in each town. He also made out a check for $1,000 and asked if I had any money. "Yes, I have $800." "Fine, you may need four or five hundred dollars of your own before your expense check returns."

He stood up and said, "Go cash that check and meet me here at seven P.M. for dinner." I was amazed, I just couldn't believe it. He didn't say what the salary would be, and I didn't ask. We shook hands and I got the feeling that he knew everything he needed to know.

It was almost three P.M. when I stopped at the cashier's window at the bank. As he counted out $1,000 I asked in my thoughts, "God, are You here?" I rushed home to tell Reven about quitting the job at the shoe store and the new job. She could hardly believe what I was telling her. "When will I ever see you?" she asked. "Well, it will be Saturday around ten P.M. and Sunday every other week." Then I decided she could spend the night at the hotel when I was in San Francisco. She was glad for me, but sad in a way.

At dinner that night the program worked smoothly. He didn't have any guests. He covered reports that had to be mailed out daily after the dinner hour, including all of the day's expenses. "Money is no object, the more guests you have for lunch and dinner the better." (I was glad he did not include breakfast.) Yes! I was an executive now, working for one of the largest tobacco companies in the world. I was supposed to be a big shot.

When I explained this to Reven, she said, "Sounds like big shit to me—leave that big shot at the hotel when you come home to me." We laughed.

The next morning I checked into the Mark Hopkins Hotel. Pat was my first guest for lunch. All went well. I didn't know my new boss was at the other side of the dining room until after lunch when he approached our table. He had never met Pat before, but he was pleased that I had a guest for lunch on such short notice. He asked her how long she had known me and she said, "About two hours longer than you have." He shook his head and said, "You'll do all right, Vic. I'll see you at the Riverside in Reno for dinner Friday night." Then he handed me a credit card that was good around the world for the airlines and said, "Don't go to Paris for dinner some night." As he turned to leave he said, "Good day, big shot."

Pat smiled, got up and said, "Goodbye, big shot. Call me again sometime." I did many times. She brought business clients of hers to lunch and dinner, which helped me and her as well.

The twelve months ahead were fast-moving ones, work night and day, using airlines, limousines, taxis, and rental cars for transportation. My guests were often at ten in the evening, midnight at the Riverside in Reno. Appointments had to be made ahead of time. There were eighteen of us in the U.S. spreading the word through executives and society.

Although I ate the best of foods I lost twenty pounds that year. The experience I will never forget. It seemed my needs were always fulfilled. At the end of twelve months, the boss called me from New York City at five A.M.—they always called at that hour if they wanted to talk. This morning he just said, "Vic! The party is over. Cancel all contracts, send in all reports. All of us are being terminated on such-and-such a date. I will call you later when I come to San Francisco."

I lay there after he hung up for a moment, then said, "Oh, hell," turned over and went back to sleep and woke up at noon.

I was at the Old Demonte Hotel in Monterey. I called Reven and told her the good news. We both were so glad we cried. In a way it was a shock, but I was glad living like a rich executive was over and now had become memories of the past. Sometimes I can hear my former boss saying, "Good day" or "Good night, big shot."

8

How Do You Know, Pat?

It was good to be home, spending time with Reven and our curly brown-headed daughter. For two weeks I just lay around. I didn't try to think of anything pertaining to work.

Then one day a thought came to me: Call Pat, call Pat. When she heard my voice she said, "Vic, where have you been? What happened?" It was hard for her to believe. I told her I had no plans, told her I would be at home. She said, "Goodbye, big shot."

A few days later she called. "Vic, I'll buy you lunch tomorrow. I want to talk to you." I questioned her, but she said, "Come to lunch tomorrow." I said, "Okay, I'll be there." At lunch we reminisced about the past year. Then she sprung a new job on me. "He wants to interview someone this Friday morning at the Palace Hotel at ten. He represents a large national van lines. The job is yours, Vic. I am not sending anyone else."

"Pat," I said, "how do you know the job is mine? You have never met the man." "I just know," she insisted, "I never met your former boss either, before lunch that day. You will be there, won't you?"

On the way home I thought, "Can You hear me, God? Are You still looking out for me? What's this new job Pat is sending me on?"

But God was silent.

I met Mr. Executive Vice President of this large organization. He was an executive, but not a big shot. He liked me and my past record and I liked what he had to say about sales promotion, working with agents and their people. It was a highly paid job with all expenses paid, plus a car. Only one thing was wrong— they wanted me to cover the eleven Western states. I would be gone four weeks and in San Francisco one week. Some weekends I would be able to fly home. I thanked him for the interview and told him I had better go home and share with my wife Reven. "Fine," he said, "but why don't you bring her back and have dinner with me tonight?" "If it's okay I'll call you back when I get home," I told him.

On the way home I stopped at Pat's office to report on the job. We sat on the couch; she was very quiet and as I looked at her she seemed more beautiful than ever. She was eight years older than I, but one that would cause heads to turn when she passed by. I asked, "What's wrong, Pat?" She slid over close, put her arms around me and said, "I'm in love with you, you big dummy." She started crying. I hadn't noticed it before. I kissed her lips tenderly and said, "Pat, I'm a married man." She knew, but she couldn't help it. Since the day I knocked the books out of her hands she had been loving me in her mind all year.

"Vic," she said, "I make a lot of money here, come in with me and I'll split with you. I won't interfere with your home life that much." I told her about the job and how Reven and I were going to have dinner with him that night. She said, "Yes and you will take the job." I asked her how come she had never married. She said she could never find the right one. I promised to call her again soon for lunch. But on the way home I said, "No, not again. God, not again."

Reven and I had dinner with the gentleman and agreed I would accept the job. I would give Reven the money she needed, which seemed like security to her. I spent four weeks in the Los Angeles office training for the task that lay ahead. I would fly home each weekend. On the fifth week I started out for Phoenix, Tucson, El Paso, Albuquerque, Salt Lake City, Billings (Montana), Spokane, and Seattle. All had gone well. I was accepted with open arms by the agents I had visited. I arrived in Seattle Saturday evening on the third weekend. I thought, One more week and I'll be back home. I always kept in touch by phone three times a week. I was tired that evening when I arrived, so I lost no time driving straight to the hotel. When I went to register at the counter, there stood Pat, beaming all over. She just said, "Here is the key to our room, Vic." I couldn't believe it. I laughed and grabbed my bag and said, "Okay, Pat, let's go."

She had selected a beautiful room and made arrangements for dinner with wine and candlelight. I asked her, "How did you know, Pat? How did you know when I would arrive here?" Her only answer was "I just knew. In my mind I have been following you." And in my mind I said, God, is that possible? My answer from God was no better than Pat's. Then she said, "I had a need, you had a need, so here I am." It was a beautiful weekend. She reminded me of Jeanie back in Kansas City. I wondered about Jeanie and hoped that she was happy. I took Pat to the airport early Monday morning. When she kissed me goodbye she said, "Don't call me. I will find you when we have a need." Happily she said, "Goodbye, Vic."

That next weekend I was back home in San Francisco and glad to sleep in my own bed. For some reason each time I left San Francisco I was always in a hurry to get back again. We would do in the town, swim in the ocean, winter and summer, take in dinners at the wharf. San Francisco was home for me.

I enjoyed what I was doing. When I left home again I would drive hard to get to the next town, sometimes driving 1,200 miles in one weekend.

Sixty days had passed and I hadn't heard from Pat. I thought, that's good; maybe she's found herself a man. Two weeks later I pulled into the Cosmopolitan Hotel in Denver and as I went to check in there she was. "Here's your key, Vic." "How did you know, Pat?" Same answer—"I just know, Vic."

In the middle of the night she said, "I have something to tell you." "Yes, what is it, Pat?" "Your wife is pregnant. She will have a boy this time." "How do you know, Pat?" "I just know. You will know everything someday. I came this time, I had to be with you. I am not going to be around very long. I have dreamed it. I have seen it. There will be an accident. I'll be no more." "Pat," I said, "you can change that; it does not have to happen." The words I said made no difference. She just lay close and expressed her love for me.

When I took her to the airport Monday morning she smiled, kissed me goodbye, and said, "I will not see you again." Then she turned and disappeared into the crowd of people. I was stunned by her remark as I sat there unable to believe her. Then I jumped out and ran after her, but she had disappeared onto the plane. I returned to my work, but could not get her off my mind. Each night I blessed her and asked God to protect her.

Thursday morning I called her office and was told Pat had been killed Tuesday morning in a streetcar accident. I just sat there wondering, thinking, Why, God, why? What is our life all about?

9

Maybe God Does Answer

I was as confused as anyone could be. I remembered Pat's ability to know, and her saying someday I would know all I wanted to know. There were moments when I felt her by my side, saying, "All is well; you will know someday."

I called Reven and told her about Pat's accident and asked her to send flowers. Then I asked, "Are you pregnant, Reven?" "Yes, I think so" was her answer. "How did you know?" From that day on if I looked at a woman two months' pregnant I would know and also knew if it was a boy or girl. "You will have a boy this time, Reven." She was silent for a moment, then said, "Of course, of course I will have a boy this time." Then she gave me that questioning giggle and hung up.

My thoughts seemed to take me back to the farm again, seeking solace with all nature. Back there all growing things of the earth die in the winter, then in the spring they come back to life again. I asked God, "Is this the way with us? Does our body die, but mind and spirit move out for rest and to be born again? Is that the way it is, God? Will Pat be born again?" "Yes, Vic, you will meet her again." "God, is that You?" No answer—God was silent. The statement was so loud and clear, then silence. Just silence. Then I got a good feeling about Pat. She will be born again, I thought. Then I cried. I couldn't help it. I guess I loved her more than I knew. I had great respect for her; she knew what she wanted and was successful in her business.

37

The months ahead moved so fast. There was always so much work to do. I thanked God for work, and I liked what I was doing, on the go most of the time.

I was home for a week, working in San Francisco. This was the week our son was born. Reven was pleased, and so was I. At the hospital I was pacing the hallway when a nurse came through the door and said, "Here is your son, Vic."

I was grateful to see a perfect baby boy. Thank You, God! And thank you, Reven and Pat! How did you know it would be a boy? No answer came, but I knew she was around.

I called the president of the company I worked for the next day and told him I had a new helper now. "What do you mean, Vic?" he asked. "My wife gave birth to an eight-pound boy two nights ago," I told him. "Congratulations, Vic, that's wonderful. Why don't you stay home close to Reven for a few days? It will do you good." Then he said, "I have been thinking about you lately, Vic. Your name comes up often by the agents and they like the new ideas you have helped them to develop. The volume of business is increasing beyond our expectations. We are having a board meeting the fifteenth of the month. I would like for you to fly back and attend this meeting. We want to talk with you."

I was pleased, but scared. The following week Reven took me to the airport, kissed me goodbye, then held up her hand with two fingers crossed and said, "Good luck, Daddy-O."

When the big jet landed back east at the airport, a friend from the company was there to meet me. On the way to the hotel I said to him, "Do you know something?" He replied, "What, Vic?" "I'm scared. I've never been to a board meeting of a large company." "Vic," he said, "they love you, they want to talk with you."

I didn't sleep too much that night, but as I entered the room for the board meeting a calmness came over me. "God, are You here?" No answer. But my answer came in the meeting from the response of the board members. I was the youngest member of their organization, they said, and they were pleased. From then on it was easy. When I left three days later the president shook hands with me and said, "If you need anything out there just ask."

The next year I became so invaluable in meetings over the

U.S. that Reven didn't know when to expect me home. It seemed like I was sleeping on airplanes more than in a bed.

Then the day came when Reven said, "Vic, I have had enough. You have a family now, we need you at home." That night at midnight I slipped out of bed and went to the living room to think about God. I sat there in silence wondering what I could say to my God, who was silent.

As I sat there motionless and silent a strong thought said, It's all right, Vic. In a few weeks you will move into your lifetime job. You will be at home. Do nothing, say nothing, it will come. As I sat there a great feeling of peace and love seemed to surround me.

The next morning I told Reven what happened. I thought she would be pleased. She just said, "Yes, I know." No more was said. The next morning she said, "Goodbye, I'll keep your bed warm for you."

Five weeks passed. I was in El Paso, Texas, about ready to leave for San Diego, when my boss called from Los Angeles and said the owner of the San Francisco agency had died of a heart attack. "Leave your car there, fly to San Francisco today. I'll meet you there tomorrow. Call the president tomorrow morning."

I was not too surprised, as he had been ill for some time. I called Reven for a pickup. When I greeted her she just smiled that impish smile and was silent. Ten minutes passed before either of us spoke. Then she said, "I think you will be home for a long time." "How come, Reven?" "I just know" was all she would say.

The next morning I called the president. He knew about the agent passing on. He would not make it to the funeral. Then he asked, "What do you think will happen there? They are one of our poorest agents, Vic." "Yes," I agreed, "suppose I check it out and in a few days I'll call you back. I think the Mrs. will level with me about the business. She has worked in the office several years."

At the funeral the Mrs. asked my boss and me to come to the office the next day. We arrived there the next morning and were invited into her office. She told us her husband had been ailing for a long time and they had already made plans to close out the business and had leased the building out. They had to be out in 120 days. They had planned to call us in a few days and explain the purpose of their future plans. When we left, my boss said to me, "Now what'll we do?"

At his hotel we discussed several possibilities, but none seemed satisfactory. Then the words started coming from my mouth: "Why don't I start a new agency? I have some money saved. I'll sell the house, find a building. It will take less than 120 days. I think we can be in business in 60 days."

He looked at me and said, "You are too important to us out there in the field." "Yes," I said, "but Reven wants me home. She wants me to quit." He picked up the phone, called the president and gave him the story about the agent. Then he said, "Vic wants to become our agent here. His wife wants him home now. He can't be away much longer." "What's your number there? I'll call you back in one hour. I had better discuss this with the Chairman of the Board. Don't leave, I may be able to call back sooner," the president said.

I paced the floor for ten minutes, then a calm came over me and a thought that said, Relax, Vic, all is well. Forty-five minutes passed before the phone rang. My boss answered, listened a minute, then handed me the phone and said it was the Chairman of the Board. I felt good now, and responded with a cheerful "Good morning, Mr. Johnson!" "Vic, how many children have you now?" he asked. "Two," I said, "and one more on the way." "Well, good," he replied, "no wonder your wife wants you at home. Now I will say it like it is. The president and I say okay, but we have to go before the board of directors. We think they will go along with our decision. We meet next week. Now you better look for a warehouse to lease. I'll sign the lease with you. You will need at least a couple of vans. We are retiring a few as we always do each year. They will be good for local work. I will ask the dispatcher to load two of them for San Francisco. We can't give them to you, but pay for them whenever you can. Maybe I had better load some packing materials in one of them. Call you next week, Vic. Good luck."

My boss couldn't believe it. I called Reven and gave her the good news. Her reply was "Maybe God does answer sometimes." The three of us had dinner that night at the wharf and rejoiced over our good fortune. When she arrived, my boss greeted her and my first words were, "You are pregnant, aren't you?" "How did you know?" was her answer.

That night at home I asked her, "How many are you planning on?" Her answer was "No more than a dozen." I dropped the subject right there.

It was about three years later when I noticed that tummy bulging out. I asked, "Hey, what is this?" She just smiled and shrugged her shoulders and walked away without any comment. It was a blond-headed boy this time. At the hospital after the delivery, when we were sure it was a boy, she asked me to call home to tell our older son that he had a baby brother. He was so glad.

The next day in the hospital room Reven told me that our son had started asking her for a baby brother over a year before. She asked him, "What if it's a girl?" "No," he said, "it will be a boy." "I didn't want another child, but he kept on insisting, so here he is," she said. The first two are brunettes, the last two blonds. I kidded her about this and her answer was "Well, you were never at home." All four of them are beautiful, wonderful people and somehow we have ended up with five beautiful grand-children—two boys and three girls. Three brunettes and two blonds.

10

Selling the Business

As I look back over the past twenty-five years and review our accomplishments, the large warehouse we built in San Francisco, the beautiful home on top of the mountain down the peninsula, many trucks, and equipment, I thank God and tell Him I could not have done it alone.

May 1, 1969, the east bay agent and I were on a plane going back east to attend the president's funeral. After the plane had reached its altitude and we had been served a cocktail, he just blurted out, "Vic, I want to buy your business." This was a shock. I knew he wanted the San Francisco area because of the national account business I had developed, but to spring it on me so bluntly made me take a big swallow from my cocktail. "Yes," he said, "I want to be sitting at your desk June 1." "Why so anxious?" I asked. "Have you a big deal cooking?" He didn't answer but just said, "I suppose I'll have to pay through the nose." My answer was "Yes, you will." He was sure of himself. He said, "Have your attorney work out the details and how we can pay you for it. I will have a check for $50,000 on your desk Monday as a partial payment. Let me know how much as soon as you can." No more was said on the trip.

June 1 he was sitting at my desk and I said, "God, what will I do now?" Then I thought maybe God was shocked too. Then I got the feeling, no, no, He helped to bring it about.

I was free of business—quite a letdown. It was hard to adjust to being idle. Memories began to haunt me: the conventions; the meetings in New York with Virgil A. Warren, ex-senator of Washington state; the times I would ask him if he would like to see a stage show. "Sure," he would say—"no tickets." "Do you want to see a show?" I would ask. "Sure, yes," he said. After dinner he would select the show and when we arrived at the ticket booth I would calmly say, "This is Mr. Warren, senator from Washington. I am Mr. Merrill from San Francisco. We would like to see your show." "Sure," the ticket person would say, "here you are, close to the front." I paid for the tickets while Virgil stood with a blank stare. This happened at least seven or eight times at different theaters. All of them would be sold out for weeks.

On one trip I took my oldest son to New York City. We had reservations home on TWA Flight 52 at five P.M. on a Friday. We arrived at the airport forty-five minutes early. We did not have time for lunch, so we stopped in the restaurant and had a sandwich. I was watching the screen listing the flights and loading time and also waiting for the call by radio announcing the loading time of each flight.

After a while it dawned on me there weren't any flights being called out, and Flight 52 had been removed from the screen. My son jumped up and said, "Let's run for it." He beat me by a block, but we were too late. The gates were closed and the plane was moving out from the loading ramp.

The big question was, what will we do now? We returned to the ticket counter of another airline, but there wasn't any space and most of the others had left thirty minutes before five P.M. It seemed impossible to get a flight westbound. We tried Chicago to L.A., but nothing was available to San Francisco.

I had ten people coming into San Francisco the next morning at ten. They were flying in from various cities. In desperation, I went over to a bench, sat down, became quiet and cried out to God. "Can You hear me, God? I have to be in San Francisco tomorrow morning."

I sat there several minutes just being silent. Then over the intercom radio system came a call for Mr. Merrill. "Mr. Merrill, come to loading ramp Flight 52." My son and I sat there; we thought we were hearing things; we couldn't understand. Then we both jumped up and ran to the ticket counter. The attendant had closed up, but he was handling some paper. He looked up and smiled, saying, "You're in luck today. Flight 52 is returning. I don't know why, but they will park over there, open up the front door and I will push the small ramp to the door. These are the regulations. I will motion you to walk out that door and climb that ramp, then you'll be on board. Good luck." We followed his instructions, boarded, found our reserved seats, and looked at each other with big broad smiles.

Ten minutes passed, the door was closed, the plane turned around and got into its takeoff position. We were in the air approximately half an hour when the captain came walking down the aisle, checking on passengers and the flight attendants to make sure all was well. When he came to where we were sitting, I stuck out my hand, shook his, and said, "Thanks, captain, for coming back for us." "Oh," he replied, "you're the two that were missing." "Yes," I said, "we were sitting in the restaurant waiting for the call. Later we were told the P.A. system was out of order." Then he told us very quietly that they were in position to take off when a red light came on the instrument panel and they couldn't get it to go off so they had to return and call for the mechanics to check it out. Then he said, "I thought we might have had to change planes. After you fellows walked through that door the light went off. We had to wait a few minutes to get clearance, so here we are." Then he stooped low and whispered, "I have had a few experiences similar to this before. I had no concern about the plane, so here we are. We'll only be about thirty minutes late." My son looked at me, shook his head, and smiled. I said, "Thanks, God, thanks."

After this experience I seemed to have a rapport with airplanes. Whenever I had to travel by plane I would visualize space on the flight I wanted and a seat was always available for me. Sometimes I would have to run to make it, but the checker seemed to know I would arrive before they closed the boarding gate.

11

Just Know You Can Do It

I was in Portland, Oregon, when Reven called about six P.M. She was very upset. Our oldest daughter, about ten years old, had just had a convulsion. Could I come home? "Yes, Reven, I will be there by morning."

I drove hard all night, 600 miles in ten hours. The sun was just coming up when I drove up to the house. All was quiet when I tiptoed in. They were all asleep. I was so exhausted I just hit the couch and was sound asleep when my daughter came in and shook me. I looked up and found myself staring into a great big smile. "Daddy!" she said, and gave me a big hug. "Are you all right?" I asked. "Yes" was her reply. "Your mother called and said you had a problem," I said. "I'm better now," she said with a smile. "Mommie tried to call you back, but you had left the hotel. We said a prayer for you. We wanted you to get home safely."

Several months passed before she had another seizure. We had prayed that it wouldn't happen again. It did, so we started our search for a cure. We could not believe it when doctors told us there wasn't any known cure for epilepsy. Reven became acquainted with a lady who worked with the Epilepsy Foundation of America. She confirmed that they had not found any cure for epilepsy.

The next two years were nightmares as the seizures became more violent and more often. Reven was upset. She had her hands full with the three smaller children. We prayed, but God didn't answer.

Then one morning our neighbor lady walked over and shared the experience they had had with their son. He also had convulsions. She gave Reven the name of their doctor and we made an appointment to see him the next day.

We followed his instructions for two months, but his drugs did not work. Then he suggested a care center in Philadelphia where she could go to school and have protection, so we gave it a try.

One month later they had it under control. She was doing great, but then something went wrong. She became a screaming, uncontrollable child. They urged us to come at once. Eight hours later we arrived in Philadelphia, grabbed a cab, and rushed to the hospital. When we arrived there, we were told she had been put to sleep with heavy drugs. They didn't know what to expect the next morning.

About eight o'clock that same night Reven said, "Vic, find Glen Clark, ask him to pray for her." I said, "Where shall I start?" She said, "At home." How did she know? He could have been anyplace in the United States. When he answered I handed the phone to her. She just said, "Glen, this is Reven from San Francisco. We are in Philadelphia, the Center for Epilepsy. Our oldest daughter is here, please pray for her. Please heal her." Glen just said, "Okay, Reven, but you and Vic go to a show or out to dinner. Please get your mind completely off her. That's all. Good night."

The next morning when they unlocked the front door, we hurried to the front desk to check on our daughter. I did not know what to expect. I believe Reven had greater faith than I, because she seemed happy. The head nurse greeted us with big smile and said, "Come, something has happened to your daughter. She's dressed and waiting to see you." When we walked through the door there she was, happy, beautiful, just as if nothing had ever happened.

We knelt on our knees that night and thanked God and Glen

for the healing that took place. The healing was complete; she never had another seizure.

Arriving home, I began to think. I had many questions. If Glen can do this, why can't others? What can't I? God, where do I begin? I do not believe a miracle happened. The laws of nature and love must have a great deal to do with healing, plus a sincere desire to be filled with God's love and become a part of this infinite source that relates to the minds of man.

Camps Farthest Out (C.F.O.) was scheduled for a meeting in Redlands, California, in June. Glen was the speaker. Reven and I attended that meeting—no one could have kept us away.

The second day I was able to sit with Glen. He knew my heart was full of questions. The main one was why can't the people in the C.F.O. camps do healing? He smiled and said, "Vic, you can; it takes practice, believing, and a desire to help another. Soon the source will be helping you. Don't question everything about the one who has a need. Just know you can do it." He made it sound so easy, but I followed his advice.

Today, many years later, I don't want to know all of the negative thoughts of those who seek my help. Now when I look at a person's body I am shown little light darts that tell me where the problem or problems are. The light and energy from my mind and hands go to work along with the help of the infinite source of God.

What happens? I just know everything will be all right. Some people will not accept healing. I do not ask why. I am sure most of them do not know why.

Reven and I returned home refreshed, filled with love and greater understanding. A friend of mine I had met at a C.F.O. camp called and said she had a friend and insisted I meet this person. I was invited to dinner, but being busy hesitated to set a date. Maybe I was scared when she mentioned E.S.P. Two attempts later we did have dinner together. This person had just started a small group that met every Monday night. For almost one year I attended the meetings. We studied together, seeing auras, receiving messages from spirits, and learning to read the future for each other. After attending those meetings I began to believe in the spirit.

Reven had acquired a sizable collection of books on E.S.P., healing, and various others that the authors claimed had been dictated by the spirits. Edgar Cayce was my favorite. I could understand and believe him. They called him the sleeping prophet. He gave several thousand readings for people in person or for people one thousand miles away. The distance apart made no difference. A record was kept of all readings and they are all on file in Virginia City, Virginia. The proof is there to study.

12

The Healing Light

I needed more experience, so I joined a group to study meditation and healing. There were about forty people, and most of them were people under thirty years of age. Although I was much older I had a great rapport with them. As we got better acquainted they asked me why a man in a business suit driving a Cadillac was attending such a group. I kidded with them and said that I was glad to see so many young people searching and they must have recognized their calling before I did.

The first practice session in healing I stood behind another student, a very lovely girl. I wondered if she would distract my attention from bringing the energy flow down about her. As I reached my hands out to direct the energy to her an astral body stood beside me nodding its approval. It was there just a second and then it was gone. In my mind I asked, Was this the spirit of Jesus? Did the pretty girl have anything to do with it?

Well, I bought her lunch and asked her if she felt or saw anything unusual. "Yes," she said, "that's why I am here. The energy flow from your hands was very strong, but there was a shadow that appeared in the shape of a man. I do not know who or what, but it seemed to be nodding approval of your first attempt in healing."

Many things happened after that relating to healing. The class was over, but I had to know more. I thought the people working in healing would know. Katherine Kuhlman told me, "I don't know. I don't know why some are healed and some are not. When

I appear before the people who are seeking help, I feel that the great love brought about by the music, the big audience (some 8,000) help to bring some healings about. I stand in the wings before my appearance at the podium as the choir sings and pray to God that all those that are seeking healing will be healed. I know many of them will be healed on the way home and many days after they return to their homes. I wish I knew the mystery of it all."

She had great power. I have been touched by her on the stage, by her two forefingers. I felt nothing, but lost all consciousness. Two men laid me down on the floor. In thirty seconds I was up feeling fine, but not knowing what happened. There were approximately one hundred people who walked on the stage and received the same treatment as I did, but they did not know what happened. This experience did not prove to me that it was a good demonstration. No healing took place. I wondered why she did not use the power she had for healing. She did not know and always said, "God does the healing."

I visited Oral Roberts twice at the Oral Roberts University. He seemed to think that God used him to bring light to the one receiving healing. The light sparked something within the person who had asked for a healing. But he, too, wasn't sure.

A friend of mine called me on Sunday afternoon one day. She lived in Los Gatos. She asked if I would come to Los Altos and help a lady healer. We would be working with five children from Stanford Hospital. They had leukemia and ranged in age from three to ten years old. "Sure, I'll be there at ten A.M." I was pleased that she asked me. The first child's name was Chadwick, five years old, very thin. He had lost his hair. He carried a little Bible and showed me a picture of Jesus and said to me, "Jesus will make me well." His mother said he had a tumor in his tummy. He would be operated on that coming Friday. I could see the tumor. It was about the size of a small chicken egg. Chadwick lay down on his tummy on the floor between the lady healer and myself. I asked my source for light and energy to flow through his body. I don't know what the other healer did. He only lay there three or four minutes when an astral body stood beside me saying,

"That is enough, Vic, that is enough. It is done." I stood up and explained what had happened, but no one had seen the astral body. It seemed to me like it was Jesus the Christ.

We worked on the other children and were pleased when we later learned three out of the five had been healed.

Wednesday that same week I went to the hospital to follow up. They had X-rays taken of Chadwick—his tumor had disappeared. He did not have the operation. Two weeks later they took him home. The other two girls stayed on for one month before being released.

One older girl about thirteen seemed to be getting along so nicely, but then had a relapse. When I first met her mother at the hospital I thought, "God, I had better stay away from this one." She seemed to have everything in the right place and the face and hair to go with it. When I left the hospital she asked me if I was coming back. I told her yes, tomorrow at ten o'clock.

When I drove in the parking lot the next day she was waiting for me. When I stopped she opened the door, jumped in, and asked if I would like to talk a bit. I said, "Okay, start talking, I'll listen." But she wanted to know about me, question after question. Then she asked if I was going to take a trip that summer. "Yes, I want go to England this summer," I said. "Have you been to England?" "No, but I would like to go with you," she said.

I looked over to the children's area and was surprised to see her daughter looking out a window at us. I suggested that we go in now as we had been there ten minutes and I had promised others that I would be there by ten A.M. Inside the hospital the daughter would not speak to me. I could feel the rage of hate and jealousy she projected toward her mother.

I knew then the cause of her illness. You can believe if one has an illness you had better look for the problem causing it. Take care of the problem and the mind will heal the body.

I returned to the hospital several times, but this young girl would not speak to me. Three weeks later she died. Sometimes people are just not aware what their actions are doing to their children. I never talked to the mother again after we had the conversation in the car. She avoided me. I am sure she knew the cause of her daughter's illness and death.

A healer is not permitted to work in a hospital unless invited by the parents. The mothers would cover up for me. A little red-headed girl about six was so lovely. I was told the mother had left home about one year earlier. The father lived in San Jose and came to see his daughter about once a month. One of the mothers pointed her out to me and suggested I try to help her. When I sat down on her bed and said, "Hi! What's your name?" she said, "Mary is my name. You're Vic, aren't you?" "Yes," I replied, "I am Vic. Maybe I can help you to get well." Then she told me she was afraid she would die in her sleep. It was hard for me to understand those big brown searching eyes. How could her mother run off and leave her?

The following week I went to see her. As I drove past the shopping center a thought came to me to get Mary a book. The Emporium was just to my left, so I turned in and went to their book department. Horses, I thought. I asked the clerk if she had some nice books with colored pictures of horses. "Yes," she said, "I have one, a very special one. Just a moment." She took about ten steps, then returned with a very lovely picture book of horses. The price said $15.00—wow! It *should* be very special. I bought it and took it straight to Mary. I was her friend from then on.

About three weeks later, about two A.M., I heard someone saying, "Vic, Vic, it's me, Mary." I sat up, trying to get awake. I said, "Mary." She said, "Yes, it's me. I'm lost. What shall I do?" When she said she was lost I knew it was her spirit speaking to me. "What shall I do, Vic?" "Oh, come here, Mary, sit in the palm of my hand," I said. "Someone will come for you in a minute or so. You will not be lonely or lost anymore." "Thanks, Vic," she said. Just then a spirit force came and took her away. She was gone. No more than thirty seconds later she returned saying, "Vic, oh, Vic, I forgot to say thank you for the beautiful book. It was the nicest gift I had ever received. Good-bye, Vic." Tears filled my eyes as I thought of this beautiful child with the big brown eyes and the long red curls.

Why, God? Why did she have to go? God didn't answer, but

there must have been a reason. Why wasn't she healed? I wish I knew. She might be living today.

Experiences, so many beautiful experiences. When I would leave the hospital after working with the children a place in my left cheek would crack and bleed. It looked like a scratch from a long fingernail.

What does the healing light and energy do? I don't know for sure, but I think it stimulates the blood cells and the atoms in the body, which causes a renewal to take place. All blood cells and atoms are renewed every seven years, so the oldest one ever gets is seven years old.

In the fall I was invited to a retreat at Asolimar, near Monterey. That evening the minister leading the retreat came to me and said that a lady standing in the back reading or looking at a book had asked him about two hours ago whether he thought I would talk with her. She didn't say what about. She looked about fifty years young. He assured her I would and asked that I not forget.

The next morning I came in late. The people were singing and she was sitting in the back row. I went in and sat down beside her. I said, "Good morning," and picked up a book and sang with the rest of the people. The next song they sang was "He Touched Me." As we stood up I told her that I was going to touch the back of her neck with my left hand. I said, "You will not feel a thing." When we sat down after the song she said, "Thanks." No more was said between us.

When the service was over she got up and hurried out the door. I didn't think much about it. I thought we could talk sometime later.

The next afternoon the minister asked me what I had said to the lady. I told him what had happened. He informed me that she had checked out of her room shortly after yesterday's morning service. We laughed when he said, "You'd better be careful who you touch, Vic." It seemed like a mystery in a way. She had not spoken to anyone, just checked out and left.

Well, the mystery was solved almost one year later. A lady friend of mine asked me to give two lectures to a group of people in their church on different dates. At the end of the first lecture a lady stood and said, "I have something to share with you." She told about attending the meeting in Asolimar, about me placing my hand on the back of her neck when they sang "He Touched Me." "Something happened when he touched me. He said I would not feel anything, but I did. When the service was over I turned and hurried out of there. I did not even stop to thank Vic. I checked out and hurried home.

"I had no idea what was taking place. I had no pain, but my head seemed to be going around and around. I went to bed when I arrived home. The next day I felt wonderful. I had a lot of strength. I did not go to see my doctor for several days. I felt better than I had felt for several years. You see, I had cancer of the spine. The doctors told me I had six months to live. Three of them were left when I went to the retreat.

"I finally got up enough courage to go to the doctor. He listened, then suggested X rays be taken. After the X rays were taken I dressed and waited for the doctor to come back in. I prayed to God to help me to become well. I didn't want to die.

"The doctor walked in holding the old X ray and the one they had just taken. He was all smiles. Then I knew I had been healed. All signs of cancer had disappeared."

She cried. I went to her, hugged her, then I cried, and soon the whole audience was crying. Between her sobs she tried to tell me she didn't know where to look for me to thank me. She heard about the meeting and she had to come to tell me. We all dried our tears, sang praise to God, and adjourned the meeting.

What happened? I don't know, and if you ask God, He probably will not answer you.

In 1978 I went to Tahoe with two of my grandchildren to teach them how to ski. The day was filled with much fun plus bruises. At ten P.M. we had pulled our skis off and started to the car. I stepped in a hole. The right ankle popped like a rifle shot. I had little pain if I held it up, so with the help of two grandchildren, ten and thirteen years, I made it to the car. We drove to Sacramento and went to my daughter's house for the night. I did not have too much pain until I took the boot off. Then the pain was the worst I had ever experienced. I knew then it was broken. It was midnight and raining. Should I go to the hospital? I stretched out on a bed and told them I would wait until morning.

A few minutes after I laid down a little spirit in my mind said, God can heal your ankle. Ask God to heal your ankle. Did I? Of course I did. Then I went to sleep—sound asleep. The next morning I woke up at seven A.M. I had no pain. I could wiggle my toes. Then I thought, could it be? I'll try to stand up and see. No pain. Shall I take a step? Yes, I'll step down on it. There was no pain, so I took several steps. I dressed and said, "Now the real test will come when I try to put the boot on. If I can get the boot on and walk I will know it has been healed." Praise God—it worked!

13

A New Business Venture

Travel was fun for me if I had a purpose, but, without one, rather dull. The last half of 1969 we went to Europe. Then in the spring of 1970 we took a cruise on a ship down through the canal over to several islands, then back to Miami and home to San Francisco.

Fun, but boring—I had no purpose. In fact, I had had it. I couldn't stand being idle. I started checking the papers for some kind of business to buy. One morning about two A.M. I was awake thinking about the future. I did not have to work, but what would life be like if I could not work? So I turned to God. God, what shall I do?

That weekend I checked the want ads again. There were three mobile home sales lots advertised in Sacramento. "Looks good to me," I told Reven. "It will be something to do." I called and made an appointment for Monday afternoon to talk to the owner. I was pleased. I liked it. God, what do You think? He was silent, as always.

It took thirty days to get everything set up, such as licenses, financing, flooring, establishing half-a-million-dollar credit line, and moving to Sacramento.

I lived on one of the lots in a nice large mobile home. Reven would come up and stay a few days, then return to the peninsula.

This to me was real fun. I had time to read a lot, practice concentrating, seeing auras, seeing people over the telephone, seeing their home, astral travel, along with learning how to control my mind. I developed a closer relationship with customers. I knew what their real needs were.

So many things happened. People's spirits started coming to me for help in the middle of the night. The spirit voices would call in thought, "Vic, help us." Sometimes there would be fifty or more lined up asking for help. It seemed each one would be asking for the one they were assigned to live with. I would bless each one and ask my God source to help them.

A friend of mine called one evening and asked my help for Mary. She was young, married, and her husband was out of work. The rent was due and their car's brakes were out. She was ready to give up. She actually needed $400. It seemed to her like a hopeless case. "Okay," I told my lovely friend, "I will give it to God." "Vic," she said, "Mary needs help, now, tomorrow." "All right, all right." So I spent five minutes manifesting, seeing, and asking God to help her.

The next morning she went to work, not knowing what to do. She was hoping to see my friend, Kathy, first thing, but instead she ran right into her sales manager. He said, "Mary, come into my office for a minute." Inside he said, "What is wrong with you, Mary? You are not like the Mary we know. What's wrong?"

Mary shared her problem with him, then he excused himself, saying, "I will be right back." When he returned to his office he said, "Mary, I can advance you $400 against commissions." How did he know she needed $400? Her mind was on her need for $400. Those thoughts transferred to his mind and he got the feeling she needed the $400.

By going into the lower Alpha levels of the mind one begins to learn how to control the thoughts of the mind. Try believing you are what you think. It seems to me that controlling one's thoughts and directing them on fulfilling one's desires brings them about. They begin to turn into actual experiences.

I'll never forget the experience I had with the bank in Sacramento the second year there. I had a flowering credit line of half a million dollars owing to cover the stock on our sales lots.

Our sales made on mobile homes were to individual people, most of them financed through our bank. To participate in this financially the bank extended the monies to cover flooring the stock at a nominal rate. The savings and loan became interested in this business, lowered their rates, and extended the financing period five years, and within six months they had eighty percent of the business.

This disturbed my banker. He appeared on our sales lot one Monday morning demanding that I press harder to retain this business or he would cancel our flooring. I politely told him I had done business with his bank for thirty years and they never had made such demands on me and I thought I was too old to start making concessions to my bankers. His answer was "Fine, that's all right, I'll cancel your flooring. You have thirty days to replace it. Goodbye." He walked over to his car, turned back and said, "I will confirm the cancellation by letter."

I stood there stunned. Where would I replace the half-million-dollar credit line, I thought. As I walked back to the office I said, "God, where will I get a half a million dollars? God, can You hear me?"

I went to my office and as I sat at my desk, I went into my lower Alpha state and thought, God, I need half a million dollars.

This was 9:30 A.M. Monday morning. At 11:00 A.M. another banker called and invited me to lunch. He asked for our business, including the flooring. When we parted after lunch he said he would call me later. About 4:00 P.M. the same day another banker called and invited me to breakfast the next morning. He also wanted our business. The third day the first banker was at my office working out details for him to take over our flooring and financing at the competitive rate. On Friday the same week he walked in to my banker with a check for a half a million dollars to take over our accounts.

I did not make one phone call. I only sat at my desk and reached out to this Infinite Source Spirit of God.

In July 1973 a thought came into my mind, saying, Sell out.

What shall I do, I thought. Nothing, came back another thought.

Three weeks later the man I purchased the business from came in and wanted to buy the big lot back. He was homesick for the place. It took two weeks of arguing back and forth to get my price.

In September two of my sales people purchased the other big lot. They found a wealthy lady to back them. The third one I closed as the lease was up anyway. So by the end of December I was out of the mobile home business and back on the peninsula. I did not make a phone call or contact anyone regarding the sale.

In 1974 many of the mobile home manufacturers closed up and many dealers went broke. How did my source know how to protect me? Sometimes I think I would like to know what and why. But then I think what's the difference who it is and how it works? I know it is related to the spirit world and God the Almighty.

In February 1974, my mother died. She was ninety-one years young. In December 1970 she called me, saying, "I want to talk to you. I am not well." "Okay, Mother," I told her, "we'll be with you Friday evening." I had not been told she wasn't feeling well. We arrived about 7:30 P.M. and Mother was lying on the couch. She sat up and told us that she had cancer of the uterus and they wanted to start cobalt treatments Monday morning.

I asked, "Why didn't you tell me before?" "Well," she said, "I thought it would go away, besides I didn't want to worry you." I wanted to cry for her, but I laughed with her. I asked if she wanted to move on to the spirit world. Her answer was "No, no, I want to be here when the great-great-grandchildren will be born. Three of them," she told me.

I moved a straight chair close to the couch, helped Mother onto it, asked Reven to help, then turned my thoughts to God.

I think He knew.

We brought the light, energy, and love to her and she was very relaxed afterwards. She excused herself and went to bed.

The next morning about eight-thirty Jack, my stepfather, and Reven were in the kitchen getting some breakfast. Fifteen minutes later Mother showed up all dressed and fit as a fiddle. I said to her, "You look fantastic. How do you feel?" "Fine, I'll help them get the breakfast."

After breakfast she said she wasn't taking any cobalt treatment, as she felt fine. She would call the doctor and tell him so. We left about three P.M. to return home, but I called every day. She continued to say she felt fine.

It took her doctor six weeks to get her to come in for an examination. He found no sign of cancer; her desire to live helped her to cure the cancer that developed within her. Why did it come in the first place? I don't know—malfunction of the flow of blood in the area, or one of the other things, such as unhappiness, loneliness, which often bring on illness.

Three years later she was tired and was ready to move on. She did not want my help. After the funeral I headed south to the desert house. I spent two weeks alone, but not alone. I relaxed, read several books, and just felt one with all creation.

The spirit world seemed to open up there in the quiet of the night. It was hard for me to believe how the spirits can communicate with one by thought force.

14

||||||||||||||||||||||||||||||||||||||||||||||||||||||||||||||||||||||||||||||||||||||||||||||||||||||||||||||||||||||||||||||

The Abundance of Life
Is All About Us

It was the summertime of 1975. Reven had taken two grand-children and gone to the desert house. I was idle and going nuts. At three A.M. something awakened me. I was startled, thinking someone was there. All was silent for two or three minutes, then thoughts started coming in. Sorry to disturb you, I cannot tell time. I suggest you redecorate the house inside and out. You will want to sell in the next year or so. As I lay I thought, Sure, why not? We didn't need such a big place anymore. Besides, I had enough beautiful carpeting that I had brought from Sacramento to recarpet the whole house.

In the fall of 1976 the house had been redecorated and was sold by the end of the year. We lived there twenty-five years. The market was high, so we bought three houses and sold them in two and a half years. When each house was ready for sale my source would bring the right buyer for the house. We have lived in this lovely home now for sixteen months. I was told a few nights ago they will have a buyer for it when I am ready.

A lady friend in the real estate business, upper peninsula, called me five times in three years saying she just had to sell a certain house. I asked my source to help her out. Each time the property was sold in five days or less. Just thirty days ago, my youngest son called and wanted help in selling a four-plex in

61

Sunnyvale. He needed to cash out, but real estate people said it would be tough—possible rent control, high interest rates, no action in the past thirty days.

I got the address, drove there to see the building and, while there, asked my source to bring us a buyer. Four days later a lady put a deposit on the building and signed a purchase agreement.

In November my oldest son and I purchased a new 12,000 square foot warehouse in Hayward to lease and on speculation. It had not been built yet, but we thought it would be a good investment. Six months ago the financing was right, as well as the price. The building would not be completed until mid-September.

The first of May the real estate salesman called and said the new building would be completed by August 15. "Okay, that's fine," I replied, "when can you meet me there? I want to take a look." A few days later we met at the building and I suggested that he start looking for someone to lease it. His reply was "It's too early." I didn't think so, and he agreed he would start advertising the next month.

When I got in my car to leave I just said, "God, I need a tenant to lease our new building." That was all. Six days later the real estate man called back to tell me they had a very promising tenant for our building. I said, "Yes, I know."

I give you these examples to help you to understand that the abundance of life is all about us. So, get your mind in order and ask for your needs to be fulfilled.

My God source helps me in all walks of life, and it can do the same for you. Example: October 1977 our big warehouse in San Francisco became available for lease. I contacted several large commercial real estate companies and gave them all the information. The largest one said my price of $4,000 a month was too high. In fact, he said, there was much space available now and I would be lucky to get $3,000 a month and I might not find a tenant for a year. I thanked him and told him that was my price and it might be best if I did not deal with his company.

He put doubt in my mind, so I had to meditate to reestablish my belief that my price was right and that there was a company that was right for my building.

By visualizing and knowing there is a need, it helps me to bring it about. It's not just for me, it's also for those that have a need for what I have. It works both ways.

In November a real estate company brought a prospective tenant to the warehouse for them to see. She called me at home, asked several questions and kept on talking, not giving me a chance to answer one of them. The most important issue was the rent of $4,000.

Three days later she called and asked me to meet with them in San Francisco the following morning. That night I asked God to help me bring it about. All went well and they liked the building, but they needed more office space. They agreed to lease the building for five years and pay $4,500 per month, provided I would install $30,000 more office space, plus a five-year option.

I did not lose one penny on rent, because I knew someone needed the building. How? Because I knew. Now! Remember this: You are you. You are the one that has to take the action, so do what is best for you. If it does not work, try again and again. Meditate; some of you have taken Transcendental Meditation (T.M.) —it is good, so carry it no further. I have studied Silva Mind Control, Alpha Dianetics, T.M., Psi Biotics, healing classes, seances, hypnotism, out-of-body travel, and have also read many, many books on parapsychology, E.S.P., and trance messages. So if you have a real desire and search for it you will bring it about.

There are several hundred books on the above subject. They will help you out. It's not all that difficult to do—it does require discipline, patience, and persistence. So do something about it every day. Do I pray when I ask? No, I just visualize, feel grateful, and ask God to help me bring it about. Everything we need is already there. Everything that is, always has been. If you love yourself and your brother as much as yourself, God will make it easier to bring about.

15

Helping People

How can we help people? We can't unless they ask or you feel they are searching for improvement.

For every person all the events of your life are there because you have drawn them there. What you choose to do with them is up to you. If you are still alive, your mission on this earth is not yet finished.

I do not like to be lectured to and I do not believe in lecturing to others. That is why I have tried to just share the experiences of my life with you.

It is easy for me to sit and get a flashback of any part of my life from childhood to the present. What man desires is already within him, but he wanders here and there searching. He stands alone, not knowing he is not alone.

People from all walks of life are searching, asking who and what is God—why am I here? Jesus said, Look within, pray in secret, ask for what you want. To me God is a spirit source. It is a part of me and I am a part of it. We are one. I am that I am.

Mind is power; it relates to the infinite spirit source, if one trains it to do so. The mind will accept whatever one chooses to give it. It's a part of all creation.

We are never given a wish without the power to make it come true. We may have to work for it, however, and sometimes we have to fight for what we want, but make sure it does not affect your brother.

Thought—the silent way to communication. The spirit force about every person relates to a higher source and manifests thoughts in man's mind by way of intuition.

When man develops to the extent that he can accept himself and God as oneness and a part of the whole (all life), then he begins to develop the qualities of sincerity and of love.

You have doubts? Of course, it's natural. But you can overcome being a doubting Thomas. Patting oneself on the back will not push you forward.

Believe you are here to enjoy and love life. Your mind is all power, but it needs direction. If you want to improve your life, set a daily pattern of meditating fifteen minutes in the morning and evening, relaxing, loving yourself and all creation.

The infinite spirit forces tell me love is the most powerful force upon the earth. Did you read in the newspaper about the three hundred transcendental meditation (T.M.) practitioners who set out to turn the tiny state of Rhode Island into a better place to live by meditating twice a day?

Groups of people were meditating in different areas of the state, just loving people June through September. The result— murder, traffic deaths, and suicides dropped 45 to 50 percent. Total deaths dropped by 11 percent.

What a beautiful lesson for all of us! There is so much to do, it's hard to find a starting place.

It was November 15, 1978, when we moved into this home in Morgan Hill. After the pool was built and landscaping done, I had a great deal of time on my hands.

I became more involved with the spirit forces, sometimes three to four hours a day. There are millions of spirits wherever there are people. When one learns to talk with them there is always a large audience wanting to listen.

One morning at two A.M. I was dreaming of President Anwar Sadat of Egypt. It seemed I was in his presence and we were talking about Prime Minister Begin of Israel. President Sadat was having a difficult time negotiating a peace treaty between the two counties.

The next night about the same hour I was awakened by someone saying "Vic." As I sat up I was greeted by a spirit that said he had talked with me the night before. He was the high spirit of Sadat. He had about two hundred spirits with him and they were anxious to help. What could they do?

Prime Minister Begin had broken off negotiations with President Sadat—there was a stalemate. The next few nights we had several sessions. I found I could go to Egypt in my astral body quickly and effortlessly. During the meetings one little spirit kept saying, "We can love them." Its message finally sank in and we accepted the idea.

After ten days of sending much love by thousands of spirits to Prime Minister Begin and his cabinet, Begin contacted President Sadat and asked to renew the talks. We continued our spirit love program through all negotiations, including Camp David and the signing of the first treaty.

I was pleased because I learned one beautiful lesson. Do not take sides or judge another nation. If I was asked to give an opinion on a situation I would say, "It might be best to turn the other cheek. To God we are all brothers, you know."

A few months later the American Embassy in Iran was raided by college students and approximately seventy employees of the Embassy were held hostage. Seven days after the raid I talked to the high spirit of the Ayatollah Khomeini. I asked if he could communicate with Khomeini sometime about some things.

I hold him that Khomeini was a great spirt of God, and God was a God of love. Maybe he had overlooked the friendship with our nation and I did not think God would hold our people hostage. The next two weeks we had many spirits loving him and the guards at the Embassy. It seemed to me there was more unrest within the nation as a whole than we realized.

Then I was surprised to hear that thirteen hostages had been released. I thanked God and asked what to do next. God was silent, so I thought it best to also become silent as far as Iran was concerned.

My thoughts go back to the state of Rhode Island and the three hundred practitioners meditating each day, sending out love each day. What if we had one thousand dedicated T.M. people? We might change many things in this world if we could love enough. How about it, God?

16

██

Lucky Me—Another Jackpot

Going back several years, while in the vanline business, each
year we attended national conventions in various cities in northern America. One year a convention was held in Las Vegas, and
Reven, our oldest son, and second daughter went with me. Over
1,500 people attended. It was a week of work and not much fun.
I had spent the first day in meetings and was somewhat exhausted
when we closed the last session.

When I stepped off the elevator I noticed Reven and two
friends in the slot machine area, so I walked over and asked,
"Are you winning?" Their response was "What time is it?" When
I told them it was five o'clock, Reven said, "We'd better go; the
cocktail hour starts at six-thirty and the dinner show is at eight."

As we were leaving the area I passed a dollar slot machine. I
had three silver dollars in my pocket. Something seemed to say,
"Put your three dollars in this machine." I stopped and played
the first and second ones with reservation, but the third one hit
the $150 jackpot. The three gals were amazed. I had little time to
play during the week, but every time I played the dollar machine
I would hit the $150 jackpot on the third or fifth dollar placed.

I had often played keno, but never won a penny. One day at
lunch a thought came: Have the waitress play a keno ticket for
you. Unusual, I thought, but I handed the waitress $15 and asked
her to mark a keno ticket for me. I asked if any of the fellows at

my table wanted to share the ticket with me. "No, no, Vic, you can't win" was the reply.

Before lunch was over the waitress brought me $350. The one and only time I ever won on a keno ticket.

What happened in Las Vegas? I wish I knew. It seems to me the mind is far greater than any other force. It is greater than the largest computer ever built, but man has not trained it to function properly. We use only ten percent of our mind.

The Christ Jesus said, "Go within, you will find all you want to know by going within."

George Washington Carver, the man who invented over a thousand uses for the peanut, said that he got his information from the little flower he always wore in the lapel of his coat.

Sir Walter Russell became a great architect. He built four of the greatest hotels in New York City forty years ago and they are still operating today. He never went to school beyond the eighth grade. He also became one of the greatest sculptors and artists in our country. He once stated how he made it possible to create such magnificent sculpture pieces. His words were "If I want to create a work of art, I sit and think about it and the knowledge just comes to me. Then I see it, and my hands just chip away the marble I don't want."

I believe faith and belief in oneself have a great deal to do with the things we think of as supernatural.

Amazing, yes! But listen to this. Every time I have gone to Las Vegas or Reno the past twenty years, starting with twenty silver dollars I always hit a $150 jackpot. One afternoon at Harold's Club I hit five jackpots within one hour.

What happens? I don't know. When I walk by the machines something within me says, "Play that machine." Remembering back to the Las Vegas convention where it all started, one evening I saw three of my lady friends playing the roulette wheel. I walked over and had the nerve to tell one of them, a cute blond from Albuquerque, to play number 3. She did, and won. Then, "Why don't you play number 5?" She won. Then, "Best you play number 3 again," and again she won. I turned and walked away.

She gathered up all her chips, came running after me, yelling, "Vic, wait for me." Lucky? I don't think so, not if you play for fun.

Two years ago we joined a few friends in Tahoe for the New Year's party. After checking into our hotel we left to attend a cocktail party. Reven and I were walking through the lobby—I had no intention of putting a dollar in a slot machine, but a thought came in, saying, "Turn left at the next aisle, then right at the next one, take three steps, turn right facing a dollar slot machine, put in no more than three dollars." I followed the instructions, put in the first one, nothing happened, and the same with the second one. Then when I put in the third one the machine jammed and the next thought was "Wait, call the attendant." The attendant came, released the machine, and handed me the dollar. I put it back into the machine and hit the $150 jackpot. Sometimes these things come to us in hunches. If it seems real to you, follow it.

I have seen people play the slot machines hour after hour and win very little. I attended a unity retreat about one year ago at Tahoe. One afternoon I went up to Harrahs. As I walked into the slot machine area I noticed a young lady playing the quarter machine. I got a feeling she was desperate. I felt she had lost the rent money or something.

I got up enough nerve to approach her and said, "Hello, are you winning?" Her answer was "No." "That's bad," I said. "It's worse than that" was her answer. I suggested she put three quarters into the machine next to the one she was playing. She looked at me and asked, "What kind of game are you playing?" "Nothing, no games! Try it," I told her.

She put in her three quarters, pulled the handle, and hit it for $500. I don't think I have seen anyone as excited as she was. Somehow I felt that she had a real need. So that need was taken care of. I do not know what the odds are on slot machines. They can be set to pay the percentage of payouts that the casinos want. But the amazing thing to me is there are 1,300 moving parts in a slot machine. Can you believe that is a small amount compared to the millions of tiny atoms in the brain? The brain is linked to the infinite intelligent source of God, which enables you to receive unlimited power. It depends upon you and what you want. Man chooses the path he wishes to follow. It is our choice to be happy or unhappy, to be positive or negative in our thinking. Happiness and positive thinking will fill our being, our soul with love, and love brings in a greater flow of energy. This energy will lift you up and the mind begins to function with greater ease. By going into one's lower Alpha and meditating a few minutes each morning and evening, it helps one to control the mind.

The mind is there to serve and it returns what you feed it. It's somewhat like a computer—what you put in you get back. Try to remember the mind is in tune with the infinite mind of God. It is also there to help us. All of my accomplishments come from this infinite source of God.

Learn to relax the body, the mind, listen and know, because this is truth. Know every tree, every cloud, every bird, every child, every soap bubble, yes, everything, everything is alive with God, to those who know His language. To me His language deals with the laws of love and the laws of nature. You, too, can do these things if you want, if you have the desire.

The Christ Jesus told us this two thousand years ago, ask and believe. Can You hear me, God?

Remembering back thirty years earlier. . . . One night after I had retired, I lay there unable to sleep. Thoughts took me back to the farm in Missouri. I relived those experiences of planting corn, beans, potatoes, tomatoes and watching them grow.

I watched the chickens hatch, the baby calves being born, the little lambs, pigs, but most of all the baby colts. It seemed like when their feet hit the ground they tried to stand up. As soon as they stood up they started looking for their mother's tit to nurse.

I milked the cows, fed the pigs, doing everything relating to family life on the farm. All of this seemed to be a part of the family. I began to realize these things I worked with were all a part of God's universal laws of life and laws of love, and I feel sorry for the children today who have never experienced this part of life.

I believe each and every one can accomplish his desires and be successful in the profession or business he chooses by relating to the laws of love. But first make sure you know what you want to do in this life, by planning, visualizing, manifesting it, and, most of all, believing you can do it.

17

Do You Know?

Each one of us is a spirit force with a body. The spirits use our bodies to live in for their progression state in learning. When you were born these spirit forces were assigned to your body soon after birth. The soul spirit, high conscious spirit and the subconscious spirit, plus smaller spirits, live inside the body. The high spirit lives in the head in back of the eyes; the others, one near the heart and one in the lower body center area. Outside our bodies another spirit force surrounds us. There is one big one; he has five to six helpers. These spirits give us protection, guide us, and try to help us to relate to the laws of nature. The soul spirit, before coming to us, has already chosen the course for its progression state, helping it to grow in wisdom, knowledge, and love.

Yes! I can communicate with them. They tell me sometimes families will stay together after the bodies die. They also agree to exchange with the females to give birth to a child so the next spirit related to the family can come back to earth to finish its progression state. For instance, my daughter has been her mother's mother three hundred years back. I have been my wife's husband once before in another lifetime. They tell me there is no death in spirit. There is no hell, no devil. These are stories, originating back over two thousand years ago. They say the only hell is on earth, which we create in our thoughts. If that is what we want, our spirits will help us to bring it about. The same thing with the devil.

73

So spirit is love. It is of the high infinite spirit of God working to return to this same source where it originated. Do you know, you will be more beautiful if you love yourself just as you are? Each and every one of one of us is a very special person. Of all the billions of people there are no two alike. Each person has a special beauty about them. No one is better than another, for we are all created alike. If you cannot love God, how can you love yourself? All life has feeling—the flowers, trees, all plant life, all animal life, yes, even the wind; but we do not understand their language.

One time I was standing on the grass in our front yard when I got a feeling it was telling me to get my big feet off. What did I do? One guess—I got off and apologized. Another time I was trimming a rose bush called the Prince of Peace. It always produced such beautiful roses. The colors were so perfect, the petals so soft. One particular rose was about to drop all its petals on the ground, yet it was still beautiful. I bent over to cut it off, but stopped and said in my thoughts, You are so beautiful, I don't like cutting you back. A response came back to me saying, We die to live.

There is a book written by Glen Clark on the life of George Washington Carver, as I mentioned earlier in this book. He tells about a few of the thousand uses he created for the peanut. Dr. Carver informed him he got all his information from the little flower he always wore in the lapel of his coat. Read it sometime. Maybe you, too, will talk to the flowers.

I used to be like most people, too close to the trees to see the forest. A big pine tree will pour out its energy if you will stand still under one. Hold up your hands and you will feel this energy come to you. I have held my hands up under a big pine tree for ten minutes and the tips of my fingers glowed with a tiny white light.

I have found by loving one plant, talking to it, praising it, the plant will flourish and become more beautiful. I also tried hating another plant, telling it it was ugly. It died. Do you know, this life will relate to us if we listen? It is so important for us to live in a positive loving attitude because it helps the spirit forces about us to function in light and joy, helping the body to relax, overcome stress and tension. Do you know, your mind will keep your body healthy if you will become a busy, happy person?

I had a friend who became a criminal when he was seventeen. He was a bum, slept in haystacks and railroad cars, eating anything he could find. Was he ever ill? No, he never became ill. He followed this life for several years and never had a cold. Why? I asked him. "I had peace of mind," he said. "I lived within the laws of nature."

18

My Son Richard

July 25, 1980, at four P.M. my wife called from Richard's office in San Jose. When I answered she said, "Vic, there has been an accident at the Old New Jerusalem Airport. One plane crashed. There is one fatality. I don't know if it was Richard's plane. It will take a while to find out." "Okay, Reven, I will be there in twenty minutes. Just stay there, don't leave." That twenty minutes seemed like two hours to me, and the thirty miles seemed like a hundred.

When I walked in the office several people, including my granddaughter, Valerie, were there consoling Reven. They didn't have to tell me Richard was dead. He was killed in his own plane, an accident that doesn't happen once in a thousand times. Reven confirmed that it was Richard. He had been killed instantly.

My thoughts went out to God. Why, God, why Richard? He was such a good pilot, never taking chances. I always felt safe when flying with him. God was silent; not even a thought came in.

I have never experienced the silence I felt then. It seemed like the whole spiritual world about us was silent.

More and more people came, friends of Richard's who worked at the airport. They, too, had trouble believing Richard was gone and asked why it happened to such a wonderful person. One who loved life and people, he was always helping someone. They loved him for what he stood for. Why, God, why?

About six P.M. I stepped outside the office to smoke a cigarette and be alone. Silence prevailed outside; not one airplane was in the sky, and none was taking off or landing. It seemed like the whole airport was in mourning.

As I walked I said, God, we will miss that beautiful smile. We will miss those big strong arms hugging us when he came around and his thoughts of love for us. What about his wife and daughter, God? What about them? But everything was silent, so silent.

As I turned and started back to the office a spirit said, "Dad! It is me, Rich. I am all right, I am all right. Tell Mother I am all right." Then he said, "You have always been so good to me, Dad, never interfering, listening when I wanted to talk, believing in the success of my business. Why don't you take over the business, Dad?" Then he said, "I have to go now. Tell Ronnie and Laurie I loved them very much." As he left he said, "Dad, I am coming back, I am coming back. I want you to be my dad again. Goodbye." Then I heard other spirits say, "Come, we have to go now."

Something within me seemed to tell me to speak to him now, so I called, "Rich, all is well. You are going to a beautiful place of rest. The spirits are filled with love; they will care for you. I have been there in my mind. There is no hell after life or in the spirit world. The only hell is the one we create in our minds while in our bodies on the earth." He spoke again, saying, "Thanks, Dad, I have had reservations about myself in that area."

"We love you, Richard. All is well." Then all was silent. My thoughts went out to God. I release his spirit to You, God. I give him freedom to go as I have done so many times in his life, in our togetherness as we shared the past thirty-five years of his life.

Silence prevailed again, but peace and love came to me. The greatest peace I have ever experienced. No more tears, no more sorrow. Just happiness and love for him.

Arranging the funeral seemed to be preplanned. So many people came, so many friends called from all over the country, so many cards and letters from friends we had not heard from in several years. Prayer groups we had worked in during the past thirty years called and said they were having special prayer sessions for the family and for Richard.

Yes, I felt the presence of God through these friends who loved us. Yes! God does answer in so many ways.

My thoughts often go back to the funeral. The casket had to remain closed, but on top of the casket we had a large recent picture of him with a card that read:

I no longer need the heavy form which I chose to inhabit in this incarnation. Therefore, I have discarded it. However, I still live! I AM!

All is well now, but my thoughts often go back to the statement his spirit said: "I want you to be my dad again." I have wondered if it is possible. Then I think anything is possible with God.

19

I Love You

I love you! I love you! I love you! What a beautiful feeling it is to be able to say to someone, "I love you!" It is also a beautiful feeling to say to oneself—"I love you!"

I don't think there is any way that can define the meaning of the word *love*. I believe people in all walks of life interpret it in accordance with their own experiences and relationships to all creation.

I am unable to describe it because it relates to so many areas of our lives, not only to human beings, but also to the spirit world —those that are about us and those that are in the heavens.

Love relates to animal life—the fish, the plants, the stars and the moon. To me it is the greatest force upon the earth and in the heavens.

I love you! Try saying this to yourself. I suggest you look into a mirror, into your own eyes and repeat out loud, "I love you, I love you, I love you!" You will find peace and joy within yourself and establish a thought force of love that will radiate to others.

This force of love is about in each and every one of us and we can experience it in many different ways. A few weeks ago I experienced the tremendous love of my ten-year-old grandson. He was asked to take a four-month-old poodle out of its cage to be put into the yard to play. This pup is the most wiggly little puppy I've ever seen. As he was carrying it outdoors, it wiggled out of his arms and fell to the floor, breaking its right front leg. The cries from the puppy excited us all, and Tylor was so patient and loving as he picked it up and held it close to him. But the screaming of the puppy made him put it down because of his sensitive ears. When we came in he stood there holding his hands over his ears, for he, too, was in pain. Without realizing it, his grandmother yelled at him, saying, "What have you done to the puppy?" She took one look at the leg and knew it was broken and said, "Well, we will take it to the vet," then walked out to get her purse. When she left the room, Tylor knelt down over the pup and began to sob so heavily, pouring his love out to it. When his grandmother returned she said, "Pick it up, Tylor," but he was afraid to touch it. He was afraid he might cause it more pain and just knelt there crying. I lifted him up and put my arms around him and told him everything would be all right. I picked the puppy up and put it in his arms and I could feel his pain, his love, and his uncertainty of my promise that the puppy would be all right.

In the car he held the puppy, but continued to sob. After the examination in the vet's office he was told that the vet could operate and make the puppy well. Only then did he accept the fact that the puppy would be all right as truth. When he came home, he came to me and smiled and said, "He will be all right."

Oftentimes, we have to look back over these experiences to get the feeling of the real love that exists all around us. You, too, can relive experiences that deal with love, joy, and pain.

Why don't you stop now and reflect back on experiences in your life? They may seem different to you now. You will probably have a greater understanding now than you did at the time.

I can remember when our son Richard's first child was born. He called us from the hospital, asking us to come quickly. We knew from his voice that he was troubled. When we arrived he was standing outside waiting for us. From the expression of pain on his face we knew something was wrong. He grabbed us both and hugged us and said, "The baby's little legs and arms are all deformed." We stood there, embracing each other, and we all felt a great feeling of love surrounding us. Again, in my mind I said, God, can You hear me? Richard's new baby is deformed. Let your love, God, shine upon this child and make her whole. There was great silence about us and we parted. Richard had gone back into the hospital. We went home and prayed and saw this child as perfectly formed. The next day Richard called his mother and his voice was filled with joy. He was so happy. He said to her, "A miracle has happened. God has healed the baby. She is perfect now."

Now, ten years later, she is a beautiful child, filled with much love for all of us.

Yes, God is love and, although He does not answer or speak to us, I feel that He lets His great love flow out to everyone, and especially to those who ask.

Those of you who understand my thoughts about love and what I am trying to say to you, and those of you who have had similar experiences accepting love and giving love, know the joy of real love. The simplicity of love is there for all who reach out, accepting it in full abundance.

Love is in the air, in every sight and every sound. . . .

20

We Meet Again

I was delighted the day I walked into the bank and as I waited to be served I spotted a very lovely young lady sitting at a desk in the front part of the office.

While waiting I could not take my eyes off her. She looked to be about thirty years old. She had a lovely face, thin and fair. The eyes, set deep, were bright and wide awake. They were hazel and seemed to sparkle, indicating one with love and a feeling for the unknown. Her hair was long, brown, and the ends curled about her shoulders. Every move she made reflected a beautiful personality.

When she stood up at her desk my eyes moved from the top of her head to the tip of her toes. Somehow I had a feeling of knowing her before. Could it be possible that I had known her another time on this earth?

Then a thought came in, saying, Vic, remember me, Pat. Oh, no, I thought! Pat! Yes, I told you we would meet again. Is this lovely lady you? Yes! I think I could love you all over again! Beautiful, when? She said, Goodbye, Vic, we will talk again.

It was hard for me to believe this was Pat. Thinking back it had only been less than forty years. Could it be possible for Pat to be reborn so soon after her accident?

The next time I returned to the bank I learned her name was Victoria. Victoria, I thought, what a lovely name for a lovely young lady. My thoughts took me back to the times we shared together. Although it was a short relationship I enjoyed every moment we were together. Each time I went to the bank to make deposits, she seemed to know I was there and came to the window saying, "Hello, Vic, how are things?" I was pleased and had a knowing that she was interested in developing a better acquaintance. However, I remembered the picture on her desk and thought, Pat, you have married and have a daughter. Once as I was thinking of her she came in and said, "Vic, I am not in love with him. I am not in love with him. I thought of you when we were married, and I thought it was too late. But now we can be together again."

My thoughts went out to her often and I wanted to send her flowers, to buy her nice things, to share a walk in the park, hold hands and reminisce about the nights spent at the hotels in Denver and Seattle.

No, this wasn't possible, but every time I visited the bank she came to see me. Then one day I asked her if she would like to go to lunch. I was pleased when she said yes.

Time seemed to be on my side. As the months went by the relationship between her and her husband became more cold. They began to have a lack of understanding because she was always thinking of me.

It was in April of 1980 when I invited her and her husband to join me at a pyramid meeting. Her answer was "I'll call you back." That evening she and her husband arrived on time to join me and others to experience the pyramid. They joined and future meetings were attended by her and the others, but her husband never went again. One evening when she arrived, I was alone. The music was playing a lovely song and I took her hand and we danced a few moments. Then we walked to the kitchen for a glass of wine. As I looked into her eyes she moved close and I kissed her and held her closer and closer.

Then there wasn't any question. In my heart I believed this was Pat, the one who loved me so much and shared her love with me. I think she, too, had a knowing of some past relationship and wanted to be close to me each meeting we attended, but the pyramid meetings ended and I was at a loss as to how to continue our love for each other.

Several weeks passed before we got together again and I thought it might be best, as I could remember the picture of her husband and child sitting on her desk.

I was in Arizona for a few days and her thoughts seemed to be with me much of the time, so when I returned home I called her, asking her if she had been thinking of me. Her answer was "Yes, much of the time. When can I see you again?" We made a date and when she approached me she was all smiles, with open arms. We were so glad to just stand there holding each other closely.

She expressed her love to me that night and asked if I really loved her. I know she knew I did, but she wanted me to say it. "Of course, I do." "Forever and ever?" "Yes, forever and forever. It will be a while before I can put a ring on that finger."

Then she said, "Vic, whenever you are ready to put that ring on my finger I will come to you. I love you, Vic, and I will always love you as I did before."

"Before?"

"Yes, Vic, as I loved you before. Remember?"

My thoughts turned to God. Can You hear me, God?

But God was silent. I am sure He approved.

God created love . . . with us in mind.